W9-BKU-657

GET UP AND RIDE

A HUMOROUS TRUE STORY OF TWO FRIENDS
AND A CYCLING ADVENTURE ON THE GREAT
ALLEGHENY PASSAGE AND C&O CANAL

JIM SHEA

Copyright © 2020 by Jim Shea

Illustrated by Belle Moldovan

All rights reserved.

No part of this book may be reproduced in any form or by any electronic or mechanical means, including information storage and retrieval systems, without written permission from the author, except for the use of brief quotations in a book review.

For more information, to contact the author, or to party with Marty, email GetUpRide@gmail.com

Follow the book on Facebook at: Facebook.com/GetUpandRideBook

Visit our website and sign up for our monthly newsletter for videos, stories, events and book club information: www.GetUpRide.com

ISBN: 978-1-7362606-0-9

Cover image: C&O Canal near Paw Paw, West Virginia

❀ Created with Vellum

EDITORIAL REVIEWS OF "GET UP AND RIDE"

"An adventurous tale"

— Pittsburgh Post-Gazette

"Insightful, full of tips and very humorous"

— Subaru Magazine's Favorite Book Picks

"Integrates plenty of local color and history to complement a series of mostly amusing anecdotes in presenting a narrative that tends to draw in readers pretty much immediately."

— The Almanac (Pittsburgh, PA)

"The honest start to "Get Up and Ride" leads into a journey – physical, metaphorical and humorous – along the GAP and C&O. An entertaining read."

— Uniontown Herald-Standard

"Contains sometimes hilarious accounts of Jim and Marty's adventures and the people they met. Jim also sprinkles in the history of the towns along the way... including the history of several important Civil War conflicts along the C&O Canal."

— USC Today Magazine

EDITORIAL REVIEWS (CONTINUED)

"'Get Up and Ride' is the top humorous C&O/GAP cycling adventure book of 2021!"

— Brunswick Main Street

"A true detailed GAP/C&O trail experience with humor and history."

— Meyersdale Historical Society

"A humor/adventure work with some local Connellsville color and history."

— Connellsville Daily Courier

"A collection of amazing and funny stories of encounters with people they met along the way as well as historical accounts of places on the trail."

— Cumberland Times-News

"A laugh-filled journey... the book also chronicles Shea's decades-long friendship with Marty, a sculptor and inner-city art teacher, who has taught his tech-exec brother-in-law to slow down, welcome new experiences and appreciate small moments."

— Notre Dame Magazine

For Phyllis & Jim and Lourdes & Tom, who gave us the gifts of family, faith, laughter and adventure.

Great Allegheny Passage

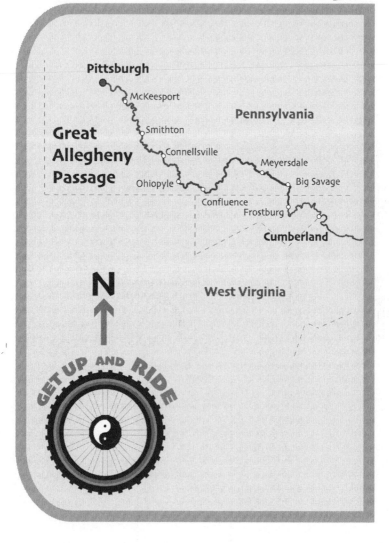

and C&O Canal Towpath

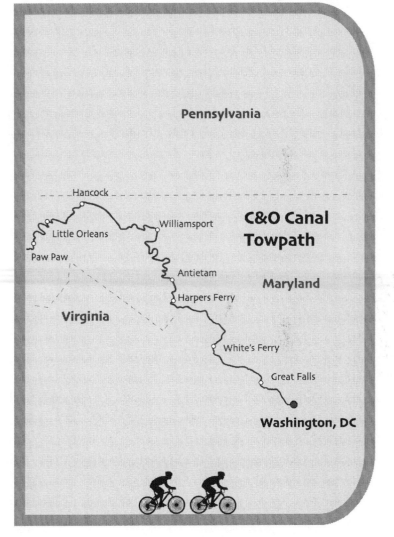

CONTENTS

FOREWORD

[To be written by Marty, once he sees what he can do]

PROLOGUE

I have never written a book or even a short story. In fact, I don't even read many books. Several people I know who regularly read books told me that books usually contain a section near the beginning which provides some background. So here we go.

I grew up in a family of four children – I have an older sister and two younger brothers. My sister was an English major and has always read a lot. I was an engineering major, focused on math and science. Not much reading was required.

Our mom would try to get my brothers and me to read, and we always resisted. We preferred to play sports and do other things. Mom often told people that my favorite book was *The Three Billy Goats Gruff* – even when I was well into my thirties. The most productive use of books my brothers and I found was to put a hardback inside the seat of our pants when we knew Mom was getting ready to spank us. Once her hand hit the hard cover, the spanking quickly stopped.

"Why don't you ever read, Jimmy?" she once asked me.

"I do, Mom. I read what I need to read – road signs, menus, e-mails, texts. I read just about every day."

When I occasionally did read a book, one thing I enjoyed was the feeling of relief and accomplishment when I'd turn a page and see the text end halfway down the next page, signaling the end of the chapter. Who doesn't love that? So I decided to design this book such that this occurs every few pages.

When I gave Mom a draft of this book to read, she said, "It's great Jimmy. Since you don't read books, you haven't been influenced by great authors such as Steinbeck or Hemingway. It reads just like you talk – it's your *own style*."

I took that as a compliment (I think).

I wrote this book to record stories that we've enjoyed telling over the years, to share the sheer joy of a five-day biking adventure, and to capture the personality of my brother-in-law, Marty, who is one of a kind. I hope you enjoy it, because – aside from changing a few of the names here and there – it's all true.

1

BU DONG (不动)

Marty and I have always enjoyed doing new things. Actually, Marty likes to come up with ideas and I carry them out. It's a symbiotic relationship.

Take this book, for example. Marty proposed that we write a book about our experience during the summer of 2010. He said it would be a great way to remember a trip we took together and to record some of the encounters we had along the way. Ten years later, I decided to write the book.

Our Chinese sister-in-law gave Marty the name *Bu Dong*, which means "not moving." And she gave me the name *Duo Dong*, which means "much moving." I like to be active, while Marty has perfected the art of being inactive.

When Marty originally suggested that we bike from Pittsburgh, Pennsylvania to Washington, DC, I was intrigued. This would mean significant movement for Marty – 335 miles to be exact. In reality, the challenge would be greater for me since Marty is an avid cyclist and I am not. Yes, although Marty rarely moves, he does ride his bike nearly every day, probably because it is one of the few physical activities one can perform while sitting.

Marty is my brother-in-law. My wife, Katie, and Marty's wife, Belle, are sisters – two of seven siblings raised in Greensburg, Pennsylvania, about an hour from Pittsburgh. I grew up in Arlington, Virginia, an affluent suburb of Washington, DC, where everyone I knew went to college. Marty grew up in a blue-collar neighborhood in Philadelphia, the first in his family to attend college.

Katie and I met as students at Notre Dame in the early 1980s. We are both engineering-oriented, left-brained people who are very methodical and logical about everything we do.

Belle and Marty, however, are artists and educators. They met at Carnegie Mellon University while studying art and remained in Pittsburgh. They are right-brained people who are driven more by emotion and feelings than by logic.

Katie and I first met Marty during one of Belle's art shows in Pittsburgh in 1985, around the time when she and Marty were starting to date. There were a lot of people around that weekend, so we didn't get to spend much time with Marty.

After we graduated from college a few months later, Katie and I moved to Maryland to start jobs as computer programmers. Belle and Marty became art teachers in Pittsburgh – Belle at a private girls' school and Marty in the Pittsburgh inner-city public school system.

I have spent my career in corporate America – in Silicon Valley, the Washington, DC area and eventually in Pittsburgh. Marty has taught art to middle and high schoolers, typically in rough areas in Pittsburgh where entering the building involves walking through a metal detector every day.

Marty is 6'1" and 230 pounds. I am 5'8" and 160 pounds.

Marty and I have known each other for thirty-five years. We couldn't be more different in terms of our backgrounds, thought processes, careers and body shapes. But we have grown close over the years, and I would trust him with my life in any situation – as long as it didn't require him to move too quickly.

PITTSBURGH

During the late 1980s, Katie and I would travel to Pittsburgh periodically to see Belle and Marty. The drive from DC to Pittsburgh is beautiful. Over the course of four hours, the flat Potomac River basin transitions to the rolling hills of Maryland and then to the Appalachian range in western Pennsylvania, with dense woods and occasional rock formations lining the highway.

Pittsburgh was hit hard with the downturn of the steel industry in the '80s, and many people were forced to move away to find jobs. In those days, Pittsburgh's struggling post-industrial economy stood in stark contrast to DC's thriving white-collar economy.

I liked visiting Pittsburgh. The bridges, rivers and hills gave the city an entirely different look than my home in the DC area. The buildings were older and the houses had character. There were ethnic neighborhoods like Bloomfield (Italian), Troy Hill (German) and Polish Hill (you guessed it). Families often remained in one neighborhood for generations. The people were friendly and would stop and talk to each other on the street. It was like stepping back in time.

Pittsburgh was also very affordable. As art teachers, Belle and Marty were able to live comfortably, which would be difficult to do in the DC area.

During these visits, as I was getting to know Pittsburgh, I also got to know Marty. He would take me to different restaurants and bars around town. One favorite was Scotty's Diner, a tiny eatery in Wilkinsburg, at that time a rough area in Pittsburgh's East End. Marty insisted that we go there after midnight so we could experience the true local flavor of the place. So, after an evening of playing cards with Katie and Belle, the girls went to bed and Marty and I headed over to Scotty's.

I opened the door and peered in. The place was abuzz, with a thick layer of cigarette smoke hanging just below the ceiling. The counter ran nearly the entire length of the diner and wrapped around the kitchen and grill. Most people were seated there. I spotted an open booth on the far end of the diner, away from everyone else, and pointed to it. Marty shook his head.

"Let's sit at the counter," he said.

We found two open stools in front of the pie case. To my left were two scantily clad women smoking cigarettes. I guessed they were working girls who hadn't found work that night. To Marty's right were four men in coveralls and work boots – they looked like they had just finished their shift. At the far end of the counter was a man with a long beard and tattered clothes, sipping a cup of coffee and talking loudly to himself. I was a bit out of my element.

Marty and I ordered breakfast – omelets with melted American cheese on top, and Scotty's specialty, Lyonnaise potatoes. We watched as the cook, known as Big Jim, worked the grill, processing multiple orders simultaneously with flawless execution. Marty chatted with the four men while I focused on my meal.

As we drove back to Marty's apartment, he wanted to know what I thought of the experience.

"What'd you think, Jimbo?"

"The food was pretty good. And that was some collection of people!"

Marty laughed. "The night scene in the 'burgh is a little different, huh? Lots of characters."

"Yeah. What was up with those four guys you were talking to?"

"They told me they just got off their shift at the machinery plant down the road. Said they're at Scotty's four or five nights a week. They said the place used to be a lot busier in the old days, before the steel industry shut down."

Over the next couple of years, Marty took me to many other Pittsburgh institutions – Chiodo's Tavern in Homestead, DeLuca's Diner in the Strip District, Vincent's Pizza in North Braddock, and Tessaro's in Bloomfield. We would experience the local flavor and always eat a heavy meal. Marty and I became good friends.

In late 1987, Katie and I became engaged and began planning our wedding for the following summer. A few months later, Belle and Marty also became engaged.

So 1988 was The Year of the Wedding for Katie's family. Their brother Thomas was married in China in February; Katie and I were married in Greensburg in July; and four weeks later in August, Belle and Marty were married in the same church. Katie and I had a formal wedding reception complete with a string quartet and seated dinner. Belle and Marty's reception was on their parents' patio, highlighted with Marty being thrown into the backyard swimming pool – in his tuxedo – by some of his college friends.

Over the next few years, we settled down and bought homes – Katie and I in Maryland; Belle and Marty in Pittsburgh. We started families and each had three sons. As in most families, our sons called me "Dad." Marty's sons called him..."Marty."

3

THE BEACH

I n 2002, Katie's family began an annual tradition of vacationing on Hatteras Island, on the southern tip of North Carolina's Outer Banks. This is a narrow slice of land in the Atlantic Ocean across which you could throw a football without trying too hard. Each time there is a hurricane, the water washes over the road and leaves less and less beach behind.

At first, Marty hated the beach. For Marty, a schoolteacher, the summer consisted of sitting on his porch, drinking cappuccinos as the neighbors strolled by, taking long rides on his bike, and working on his house. When we suggested going to the beach in North Carolina, which was a ten-hour drive from his home in Pittsburgh, Marty objected.

"Why would I leave the perfectly good vacation I have here, drive ten hours, and go to a place that is hot, with sand everywhere? And *pay* to do it?"

Marty had a good point. But Belle argued that their boys would love a beach vacation and would want to be with their cousins, and asked Marty to do it for the kids. Marty reluctantly agreed.

On the first few annual trips, Marty sulked most of the day. He went out on the beach briefly at sunrise, then came inside as it started to get hot. He watched the Tour De France on TV by day and read books in solitary confinement at night in his room. He bided his time until the week was over and then started to get excited on the last day as we packed up to head home. Marty hated the beach and couldn't wait to get back to his vacation – on his porch in Pittsburgh.

Marty is a very observant person. On our third trip to Hatteras, he started noticing the billboards as we got closer to the shore:

Your *Vacation* Starts Here

Vacation Rentals

Outer Banks *Vacation* Homes

Then he started observing the behavior of people as they arrived at the beach. He noticed that as families unpacked their cars and moved into their rental homes, they were excited and cheerful. And as they packed up and left on their last day, they were sad and more subdued.

After processing all this, Marty came out with a profound conclusion:

"Jimbo, I think for most people, this actually *is* their *vacation!*"

"Yes Marty, that is right. And I am one of those people."

Once Marty gave into this idea, he embraced the beach. Marty would go out on the beach at sunrise and never leave. He stayed on the sand for around twelve to fourteen hours, and we would need to eventually drag him in for dinner. Marty loved the beach.

Marty loving the beach at Hatteras Island, NC

We enjoy going to Hatteras Island because it is a beautiful, remote and isolated place. Looking down the beach we can see the famous Cape Hatteras Lighthouse, the tallest brick lighthouse in the U.S. at 208 feet.

The tower is situated at the southern bend of the island, only 650 miles west of Bermuda. It was used as a beacon before World War II to keep ships from running aground. During the war, the military used it as an observation tower as over sixty German U-boats were lurking just off the coast, constantly firing torpedoes at U.S. ships. More than 300 U.S. ships were sunk by the German submarines during that time, giving the area the nickname "Torpedo Junction." It was the closest that World War II came to the U.S. mainland.

The Cape Hatteras lighthouse still operates, making a full rotation every 7.5 seconds. From the top of the lighthouse, you can see the entire expanse of Hatteras Island in both directions. It is a beautiful structure with black and white diagonal stripes running around it like a huge candy cane.

Cape Hatteras Lighthouse, Buxton, NC

On our annual beach "vacation," Marty, Belle, Katie and I typically get up before sunrise and head down to the beach to watch the huge red fireball come up over the ocean, lighting up the sky with every shade of red, orange, pink and purple you can imagine. There is usually no one else on the beach, save for an occasional fisherman. Once the sun is up, the girls typically head back to the house. That leaves just Marty, me, the beach and the lighthouse. We have lots of time to talk about new things we'd like to do.

It was in the summer of 2009 on the beach, just after sunrise, when Marty first brought up the idea of doing a bike trip from Pittsburgh to Washington, DC.

The last few years had witnessed the completion of the Great Allegheny Passage (GAP), a 150-mile section of railroad-turned-bike trail connecting Pittsburgh to Cumberland, Maryland. From Cumberland, bikers get on the Chesapeake and Ohio (C&O) Canal towpath, a 185-mile trail to Georgetown in Washington.

Marty had ridden parts of this trail several times before but had never completed the entire ride. I had never done anything like it, and in fact had never ridden more than twenty-five miles on a bike in one day. I wasn't sure about the idea of having a bike seat attached to my butt for five or six days, not to mention dealing with rain, bugs, and flat tires.

I told Marty it sounded interesting but was non-committal, mainly because I had a job – a job that required me to work during the summer, except for the one week I took off to go to the beach.

4

THE WATCH

I n 2003, I was approached with a new job opportunity in Pittsburgh. Katie and I and our boys were very happy in Maryland and it was a difficult decision. It would mean leaving all our friends and family in the DC area, changing schools for our kids, and moving to a new place. But Belle and Marty lived in Pittsburgh, along with Katie's brother Andy and Katie's parents. During our many trips to Pittsburgh over the years I had grown to like the city. So ultimately we decided to make the move.

We settled in a suburban neighborhood and our sons quickly adjusted. We got together with Belle and Marty and their sons often. Marty continued teaching during the school year – taking summers off, while I worked hard at my corporate job.

Seven years later, in April 2010, my company completed an initial public offering. I had been working eighty-hour weeks for months on the project, and I was ready for a break. So I resigned from my job and decided to take a sabbatical.

Coincidentally, Marty had shoulder surgery in March

and was off all the way through the summer. So I had someone to hang out with. Marty couldn't yet ride his bike, so instead he would go on long walks. I started walking with him, and we would fill the time with inane conversation.

One warm day in late April, we went for a ten-mile walk on the Pittsburgh river trails. We started in Lawrenceville, walked down the Allegheny River, around The Point and then up the Monongahela River along the Southside. This gave us ample time to talk about nothing.

"Jimbo, now that you're off work for a while, you need to learn how to really relax."

"What do you mean?" I asked.

"Well, for starters, you need to lose track of time."

"Huh?" The Allegheny River water level was high due to the spring run-off and the trees were just starting to bud. It was a weekday and we were the only people on the trail.

"Yeah, that watch you're wearing. It needs to go. All you do is look down at it, and it reminds you of what time it is and what you need to do next. Get rid of it." Marty gestured as if he were removing something from his wrist.

"How will I make sure I'm on time for my appointments?"

"That's the point. When the sun comes up, that's the start of the day. When it goes down, that's the end. That's all you need to know."

"Okay..."

"Next, you need to lose track of days. You want to wake up in the morning and not know what day it is."

"What?"

"Yes," Marty said. "For example, I have no idea what day it is today."

"What if you have a doctor's appointment?"

"They always call and leave a message the day before to

remind you, don't they? I have never missed one." Marty was making a sound argument here.

"So you don't keep a calendar?"

"I am fifty-two years old and have never had a calendar."

We finished our walk and celebrated our accomplishment over a beer at the Hofbrauhaus, a replica of the original Munich beer hall, set on the Monongahela River. We sat outside at a picnic table with no one else around.

"Jimbo, if we did that bike trip to DC, we'd ride along the trail we just walked. We'd start at The Point and ride right past here," said Marty as he sipped his lager.

"Your shoulder is still recovering, isn't it? When are you gonna be back on the bike?"

"Should be in a couple of weeks. Would be great to do that ride this summer, Jimbo."

"Yeah... maybe," I said. I still wasn't seriously considering it as I hadn't been on a bike in years.

I said goodbye to Marty and drove home.

That night, as I was getting ready for bed, I took off my watch and placed it on my nightstand, which was my typical routine. Before I got into bed, I looked again at the watch. I picked it up off the nightstand and tucked it in my dresser drawer, deep under my T-shirts. I was not yet ready to give up the calendar, but getting rid of the watch was liberating. I have not worn a watch since that day.

SEE WHAT YOU CAN DO

Over the next month, Marty brought up the DC bike trip a few more times. I usually found a way to change the subject. By the end of May, I started giving it some serious thought. Why not? Marty had completed parts of the trip before, so he knew how to navigate it. And I thought it would be really cool to ride a bike from my current home in Pittsburgh to my boyhood home in Arlington, Virginia. Plus, I could get myself in shape, right? I told Marty I was in.

Recall that Marty is relatively inactive (except for biking). Close family members use one of Newton's Laws to describe Marty: *A Marty at rest tends to stay at rest; a Marty in motion will soon be at rest.* Marty is happiest when he is sitting.

Marty and I had talked about doing the ride in August, to ensure we experienced maximum heat and humidity, of course. One night, when Marty was over at our house for dinner, he said, "Hey Jimbo, we should probably make some reservations for the bike trip. Sometimes the hotels end up getting kind of crowded."

I replied, "Do you know of some places where we could stay?"

Marty then gave me a book about the Great Allegheny Passage and said, "Why don't you see what you can do?"

This was all I needed to spring into action.

The first thing we needed to do was nail down the dates. The fact that Marty never keeps a calendar presented a bit of a challenge here. However, Belle had recently given him an iPad for his birthday, and Marty told me he'd just realized it had a calendar in it.

When I asked Marty what dates were good for him, he opened his iPad calendar, showed me the empty screen, and said, "Jimbo, I have nothing on my calendar." That made it easy.

We picked the second week in August. I began mapping out the trip, calculating mileage between possible stopping points and researching hotels and B&Bs. I figured if I really trained hard we could ride sixty to seventy miles a day, which would mean a five-day/four-night trip. I looked at the map and picked four places to stay, made the reservations, and presented the plan to Marty.

"Hey Belle, look! Jimbo saw what he could do," said Marty.

Belle took Marty's iPad and added "Bike Trip" into the calendar from August 9-13.

"Well done, Jimbo," he said to me. "Now I have something on my calendar."

PLANNING

R iding a bike from Pittsburgh to DC is not something most people do. There are tour groups that run the trip complete with spare bikes, food and a sag wagon if you need a break. But those trips take seven or eight days and require you to stay with the group. Marty and I wanted an adventure, so we decided to go it alone.

Not many people consider the full GAP/C&O ride because it is difficult for young children; hence it does not make for a great family vacation. It can also be painful and hard work, which most people do not associate with "vacation."

The ride has two main parts. The first part is a gradual ascent over 150 miles from 700 feet elevation in Pittsburgh to 2400 feet at the Eastern Continental Divide at the top of Big Savage Mountain in Western Maryland. This is the Great Allegheny Passage (GAP), a bike trail built on former railroad tracks which winds along several rivers and has an uphill grade of one to two percent. Once you reach the top of Big Savage, the GAP goes through a long tunnel, and then descends 1800 feet over only twenty miles down to Cumberland. This rewards cyclists with nearly two hours of coasting.

From Cumberland, bikers get on the C&O Canal towpath, which is the original path mules used when pulling barges on the canal in the late 1800s. This path runs for 185 miles, descending from 600 feet elevation at Cumberland to sea level, at Georgetown in Washington, DC.

Some people start in DC and ride to Pittsburgh, but that involves riding uphill from Cumberland to the top of Big Savage Mountain. We live in Pittsburgh, so we decided we'd start there and enjoy the coasting part.

We also faced a major question: how would we get home from DC? Marty really didn't worry about these details, particularly during the summer. But I felt we needed a plan. We decided we'd stay the last night at my parents' house in Arlington, and then Katie or Belle would pick us up and drive us back to Pittsburgh.

After I'd committed to the bike trip, I quickly realized that I was ill-prepared. For starters, I didn't even own a bike, much less any of the other gear I would need for the trip.

One Saturday afternoon, Marty took me to Pittsburgh Pro Bike, a shop near my house in the South Hills. At the time, they offered three primary types of bikes – mountain bikes, road bikes and hybrids. This was before the advent of the "gravel bike," which has since become the standard for trail riding.

We quickly ruled out road bikes, as they are really designed for high-speed road riding. That left hybrids and mountain bikes. I had borrowed one of Marty's mountain bikes once before and was comfortable riding it. Also, Marty said that the rougher condition of the C&O towpath would require a more stable bike. So, I selected a mid-range mountain bike and added a set of slightly narrower tires to reduce the roll resistance.

Next came the gear. We walked over to the apparel section, where I grabbed a couple of neon yellow bike shirts with pockets sewn into the back. Marty said the bright color would help him see me more easily from a distance (more on Marty's eyesight later), and the pockets would be great for holding food for munching while riding.

Marty then showed me a rack of fingerless gloves with padding in the palms. He said the vibration of the bike over many hours can affect your hands and sometimes even make them go numb. This didn't sound like fun, so I chose a pair with the thickest padding I could find.

Next, Marty suggested I buy a pair of bike shorts with padding sewn into the seat. I lifted a pair off the shelf and looked at the padding inside.

"What kind of underwear do you wear with these?" I asked.

"None."

"What?? I don't think so..."

"Trust me, Jimbo. You are better off without anything under there. Except this." Marty grabbed a tube of "Chamois Butter" off a nearby shelf.

"What do you use that for?"

"This stuff is miracle cream. You'll be on that bike for hours – you'll be sweating, it'll rain... without it you'll be dealing with a hellacious rash after a couple of days. Butter up, Jimbo!"

I added the butter to my growing pile of merchandise.

Marty then suggested a pair of metal bars which attached to the ends of the handlebars and angled up and in towards the center. While the typical mountain biking riding position is somewhat hunched over, these bars would provide me with the option of sitting upright during long, straight stretches.

Last came the shoes. I had assumed I'd wear tennis shoes with the standard flat pedals that came with the bike. Instead, Marty said I should buy clip-in pedals and a pair of cleated biking shoes. This set-up provides for a more efficient use of your body's energy, since you are delivering power to the pedals on both your downstroke and upstroke. I went along with his suggestion and added the special shoes, cleats and pedals to my mountain of stuff.

We headed to the counter. The store manager looked at me.

"Looks like someone is getting started cycling here!"

"Yeah, we're riding the GAP this summer," I said proudly.

"Awesome, I've done it a couple of times. You'll love it." He looked at Marty. "You guys gonna train?"

"Yeah, definitely. Jimbo's gotta learn how to use these pedals first, though."

Marty's comment didn't register with me at the time.

The manager rang up my merchandise. I handed over my credit card, thinking about how to break the news to Katie that I'd just spent our savings for her new kitchen cabinets on what might be a short-lived hobby for me.

7

TRAINING

As we left the bike shop, Marty told me the manager was right – we needed to train or else the ride would be a painful experience. Marty typically bikes over a hundred miles a week, so the training was really more important for me.

To train for this ride, we needed to find a relatively flat area that would simulate the GAP trail. Marty suggested the Montour Trail, a sixty-mile stretch of crushed limestone with a gentle grade that was built on the right-of-way previously used by the Montour Railroad.

The Montour Railroad was originally constructed in 1877 to transport coal from the mines around Pittsburgh to the city's steel mills. At its height in the 1930s, the railroad served twenty-seven mines transporting nearly seven million tons of coal annually. By the 1950s most of these mines had been depleted, and in 1984, the last mine closed and the railroad shut down. In the 1990s large portions of the rights of way were acquired by the Montour Trail Council and construction of a bike trail began.

Marty and I decided the Montour Trail would be our

training ground. I can access the mid-point of the trail within a few miles of my house in Pittsburgh's South Hills, ride for thirty miles to the end at Coraopolis, then turn around and ride thirty miles back. This would give us a good way to train for the sixty-plus mile days ahead of us on the ride to DC.

On our first attempt of the trail, Marty picked me up and put my bike on his rack. We drove down to the access point and unloaded. I was wearing my new bike shirt and shorts, and I started "buttering up" while Marty installed my new clip-in pedals and screwed the cleats onto the bottoms of my new shoes. I put on the shoes and was ready to go.

"Be careful with those pedals, Jimbo, they take some getting used to. When you stop, you need to swing your foot out to pop out of the clips. Kind of like ski bindings."

"Got it."

We started on the trail, and I managed to get my cleats to clip into the pedals without too much trouble. I quickly became accustomed to the feeling of pushing down and pulling up with my feet in a circular motion. I could see how it was a lot more efficient than traditional flat pedals.

After a couple of miles, I called out to Marty, who was a few lengths ahead of me.

"Hey, I need to adjust my seat – can we pull over?"

Marty pulled off the trail, and I pulled in behind him. Just as I was coming to a stop, a feeling of panic hit me. *My feet were still attached to the pedals!* I tried to swing them out to release them, but it was too late. My bike started leaning – I was firmly clipped in and there was nothing I could do. I braced myself and went down hard on the ground.

BANG!

"You okay, Jimbo?!"

I picked myself up and brushed myself off. "Yeah, I get

what you mean about those pedals."

I got back on the bike and practiced getting in and out of the clips a few times while going slowly. After I got the hang of it, we continued on the trail.

On that first trip, I was exhausted after twenty-five miles. However, I kept at it and got stronger. Marty, of course, had no trouble at all. Every time we did a training ride, Marty would be out in front of me, sometimes for several miles. He would wait for me and I would eventually catch up. As I mentioned earlier, Marty likes to sit, so he had no problem sitting on a bench waiting for me. Once I got there, I would catch my breath for a minute, and we'd continue.

The Montour Trail is a fairly flat and straight trail which looks similar in many places. As you drone on from one end to the other, you get into a hypnotic rhythm and sometimes lose track of exactly where you are. You can just let your mind wander while your legs continue pumping along. A post marking each mile is a constant reminder of how far you have gone (or how far you have left to go). It took me seven hours to complete the entire trail the first time - thirty miles out, thirty miles back.

When you bike long distances, you get hungry - *really* hungry. After a couple of hours of riding, all you can think about is food. Marty and I would carry snack bars and munch on them as we rode, but it wasn't enough. You need to eat - *a lot*.

Marty is not a big "rules" person – he generally likes to go with the flow. But he does have a few rules for bike riding. One of them is that you are not allowed to speak about food until you are within ten miles of finishing the ride. If you talk about food too early, he says, you will drive yourself crazy and will need to stop to eat and will never finish the ride. With ten miles to go, starting to think and talk about food will give you the energy to pick up the pace and finish strong.

Marty also has a secondary rule associated with this rule: you can talk *generally* about food with ten miles to go, but with five miles left, you can get *specific*. Specifics entail talking about the exact things you plan to eat, such as the type of bread and meat in a sandwich, the condiments, and whether it is sliced diagonally or vertically. Let me give an example.

One day in May, we decided to do an evening training ride on the Montour Trail. We began around 5:00 p.m. Before we started, Marty told me that he bought a sub sandwich from Giant Eagle, the local grocery store, and that he had it in a cooler in his car. I knew we wouldn't finish riding until midnight, so I put it out of my mind for the time being.

We completed the outbound stretch in about three hours. By then it was dark, and Marty turned on his head lamp for the return trip. The beacon attached to Marty's helmet could light up Heinz Field. When he looked left or right into the woods, we would often see pairs of eyes from unknown creatures looking back at us. I didn't have a lamp, so I rode behind him and followed his lighted path. At one point, a bat dive-bombed Marty and appeared in the light stream. Riding at night was an eerie experience.

And it was getting cold. I was wearing a short-sleeved bike shirt and shorts, and the temperature had dropped to sixty degrees. With a 10 mph breeze we created by riding, it felt at least five degrees colder. I was ready to finish.

At 10:00 p.m., we had twenty miles to go. I was starving but adhered to the rule and said nothing. As each mile marker clicked off, I'd immediately anticipate the next one.

Fifteen miles to go. I needed to eat.

With ten miles left, at around 11:00 p.m. in the pitch

dark, we started talking.

"You ready for that sub, Jimbo?"

"Yes," I said, my teeth chattering.

"Me too."

That was the extent of that conversation, until I saw the five-mile marker. At that point Marty let me in on the surprise he had in store for me when we arrived.

"Let me tell you about that sub, Jimbo."

I was a little out of breath after riding fifty-five miles.

"What about it?" I huffed.

"Well, it has a name. It's called 'Three's a Crowd.'"

"What's that mean?" I was intrigued.

"Turkey, ham *and* roast beef. All together in one sandwich."

"Wow, sounds crowded." I pedaled on. "Real turkey or processed deli turkey?"

"Real turkey."

"Sliced or shaved?"

"Shaved," said Marty. "With Dijon mustard, a little mayo, lettuce, tomato, and black olives. On a massive freshly baked sub roll."

"*Oh my God.*" I could see it and taste it. I started hallucinating.

"And hot peppers, and pickles too. The works."

Three miles to go.

"I got some cold beers too. You ready for that?"

"Let's pick up the pace," I said.

We pedaled furiously to the finish line. Just before midnight, we pulled into the parking lot. As always, Marty's folding chairs were in the back of his car. He set them up, pulled out the masterpiece known as Three's a Crowd and popped open the beers. We had a midnight feast under the stars and reveled in what we had just accomplished.

❧

Most people like food. Marty *loves* food. Although he rides his bike nearly every day, he still weighs over 230 pounds. The reason is that Marty eats a lot of junk food, and likes beer.

One day during our training period, Marty suggested we mix up our training routine. He introduced me to hot yoga – he said it is a good way to stretch out your body and gain strength which helps with biking. His favorite yoga studio is on Pittsburgh's Southside, with a view of the Carson Street Deli out the window so you can watch people eating while you work out.

Hot yoga is totally intense. The room is heated to one hundred degrees. On a 3' x 5' mat, you work your way through excruciating poses and cycles of "warrior-one," "warrior-two," "up-dog," "down-dog," until you end up dog-tired. You will never sweat more or burn more calories in a fifteen square foot space than you will doing hot yoga.

When the class was finished, we rolled up our mats and walked out onto East Carson Street. Marty pointed to Piper's Pub, a bar a block away, and we headed over. Walking in, drenched with sweat, we had no problem finding a table with no one else near us. We ordered two large IPAs, quickly downed them, then ordered two more.

Then came the burgers – half a pound of perfectly cooked ground beef, piled high with bacon and a big glob of Stilton cheese. On the side was a mound of steak fries and a dill pickle. We negated the cleansing effects of our seventy-five minute yoga session in about ten minutes.

"Jimbo, if you are going to *de-toxify*, you have to *re-toxify*," Marty said. "It's all about balance."

8

GET UP AND RIDE

A s we closed in on the last few weeks before the ride, I began thinking in more detail about the trip. I am a planner and like to know details.

"Marty, I know we will have a destination for each night, but specifically what will we do each day?" I asked him.

"Get up and ride," he answered.

"That's it?"

"What else do you need to know?"

That was it as far as Marty was concerned. Get up and ride. I had already made hotel and B&B reservations for each of the four nights. Even though Marty wasn't concerned about the details, one evening I presented an itinerary anyway:

Day 1: Pittsburgh to Ohiopyle, Pennsylvania (77 miles)

- Ride the Great Allegheny Passage (GAP) trail along the Monongahela River from Pittsburgh to

McKeesport. Then follow the Youghiogheny
River to Ohiopyle.

- Pittsburgh is at 700 feet elevation while Ohiopyle
  is at 1200 feet, so our first day would involve a
  very gradual incline.
- Stay at the Ohiopyle Lodge, an apartment in the
  center of town.

Day 2: Ohiopyle to Frostburg, Maryland (58 miles)

- Follow the Youghiogheny River for ten miles to
  Confluence, Pennsylvania (1330 feet elevation).
- Past Confluence, follow the Casselman River to
  Meyersdale, Pennsylvania. Then continue on the
  GAP trail to the top of Big Savage Mountain
  (2400 feet) and ride five miles downhill to
  Frostburg, a university town at 1500 feet.
- Stay at the Trail Inn in Frostburg.

Day 3: Frostburg to Hancock, Maryland (76 miles)

- Descend from Frostburg (1500 feet) to
  Cumberland, Maryland (600 feet) over fifteen
  miles.
- At Cumberland, the GAP trail ends and the C&O
  Canal trail begins, paralleling the Potomac River.
- Ride the C&O trail to Hancock and stay at the
  Manor Inn, a Bed & Breakfast in nearby Berkeley
  Springs.

Day 4: Hancock to Harpers Ferry, West VA (63 miles)

- Return to the C&O Canal trail and ride to
  Harpers Ferry, a historic town at the confluence
  of the Potomac River and the Shenandoah River.
- Stay at the Harper Hotel.

Day 5: Harpers Ferry to Washington DC (61 miles)

- Ride the C&O trail from Harpers Ferry to
  Washington, DC. The trail ends in Georgetown.
- Ride to the Washington Mall and see some of the
  monuments; then cross the Potomac into
  Arlington, Virginia.
- Stay at my parents' house in Arlington.

Marty was pleased with the plan. I then asked Marty what we should bring. Marty is a minimalist, and he showed me the bag he planned to use. It was a small bag that strapped to a rack on the back of his bike. It could hold a pair of flip-flops, two or three T-shirts, an extra bike shirt and shorts, toiletries, and bike equipment (pump, extra tube, repair kit, etc.). He said this would be lighter and less bulky than using panniers attached to the sides of the back wheel.

I agreed to do the same. Because we had room for only one extra set of bike clothes, it would mean washing them each night and drying them out on the bike the next day as we rode along.

"Jimbo, the great thing about this trip will be all the hours you have to yourself. Just pedaling along for five days, with nothing but your own thoughts inside in your head," Marty said.

"Sounds great, Marty, but we do need to do some planning and think about some details. Like... where will we meet on the first day?"

We decided to meet at The Point, the confluence of the Monongahela and Allegheny Rivers and the centerpiece of Pittsburgh. Since I live in the suburbs and Marty lives in the city, we agreed to meet there at 7:00 a.m. on Monday, August 9th.

9

LAUNCH POINT

On Sunday night, the eve of our departure, I inspected my bike and packed my bag. I had to remove several items that wouldn't fit. Once I was down to the bare minimum, the bag weighed a total of eight pounds. I strapped it onto the small rack on the back of my bike and gave it a test run.

I didn't sleep well in anticipation of the start of the trip and was up early. I ate a big breakfast and put my bike in the back of our van. Katie and I headed into the city, arriving at The Point by 7:00 a.m.

It was a beautiful morning without a cloud in the sky. We parked by the hotel at the entrance to Point State Park. I took my bike out of the car, attached the bag and was ready to go. Where was Marty?

About fifteen minutes later, Marty appeared on his bike from around the back of the hotel and glided over to us with a big smile on his face. He had pedaled over from his house, about three miles away.

"Hey kids, you'll never guess what just happened!" Marty clearly had a story to tell.

"What?" I asked.

"As I was riding over here just now, I saw a guy coming toward me on a bike. Just before I passed him, a pigeon comes flying across and clocks him in the head. A pigeon! Hit him right on the side of his head."

"Was he okay?" Katie asked. Marty was cracking up.

"I... think so... I don't really know. I was laughing so hard. Anyway, you know it's gonna be a great day when it starts out with something like that!"

Katie and I shook our heads and couldn't help but laugh along with him.

"Well, you ready for a ride, Jimbo?" Marty asked excitedly.

"I am. Let's do it."

Katie took a picture of us as we prepared to depart.

"First let's head out to the fountain at The Point," Marty said. "We can get another picture there."

I kissed Katie goodbye, got on my bike, and Marty and I pedaled out to the tip of The Point.

Pittsburgh is known for its Three Rivers, and Point State Park is the place where the Monongahela and Allegheny Rivers converge to form the Ohio, which flows west for nearly 1000 miles to the Mississippi River.

In the mid-1700s, this spot was known as the "Forks of the Ohio" to the Ohio Company of Virginia, a group of wealthy Virginia land owners who saw the area west of Pittsburgh (the "Ohio Territory") as a strategic area for trade and settlement. Unfortunately for the Virginians, the French had the same idea.

The Virginians scored first, and in February 1754, they established a small fort here – Fort Prince George. Two months later, the French forced them out, knocked down their fort, and built a much larger structure – Fort Duquesne, which they staffed with 500 French soldiers.

Three months later, George Washington, then only twenty-two years old and a low-ranking Virginia militia officer, was sent to Pittsburgh to scout out the situation. On his way, about sixty miles southeast of Pittsburgh, he and forty of his men surprised and fired on a small contingent of French and Native Americans – the first shots of the French and Indian War.

The French responded by sending over 400 men from Fort Duquesne to attack Washington at Fort Necessity five weeks later. Washington surrendered and signed a letter (written in French, which he didn't fully understand) indicating he and his troops would back off.

The next year, in 1755, the British decided it was time to send a real army. British General Edward Braddock marched to Pittsburgh with over 2,000 British regulars, along with George Washington since he was familiar with the area.

With the help of their Native American allies, the

French got wind of Braddock's approach. About ten miles upstream from The Point, on the banks of the Monongahela at Turtle Creek, Braddock and Washington were surprised by the French and Indians. The British were decimated and Braddock was killed in the "Battle of the Monongahela," leaving Washington behind to command what was left of the regiment at the age of twenty-three.

Three years later, with the war fully underway, the British tried again. They sent General Forbes to the Forks with 6,000 men, again including Washington. The Battle of Fort Duquesne in 1758 led to the French abandoning and burning down the fort. The British rebuilt it and named it Fort Pitt, after William Pitt, the British Secretary of State.

And that is a long-winded way of explaining how Pittsburgh got its name!

~

As Marty and I stood at this site in 2010, the scene looked a little different than in 1758. The outline of the fort is still visible, but everything else is new. Across the Allegheny River we could see Heinz Field, home of the Steelers, and PNC Park, home of the Pirates. The Three Rivers Casino now sits just downstream, where the Ohio River starts. Across the Monongahela, the Station Square shopping complex forms the base of Mount Washington, while the Incline, Pittsburgh's familiar funicular, makes its way up and down the mountain several times an hour.

We took a selfie at The Point, then mounted our bikes.

"Let's do it, Jimbo!"

Marty led the way across the Smithfield Street Bridge to the bike trail on the Southside. Here we began our trip on the Great Allegheny Passage.

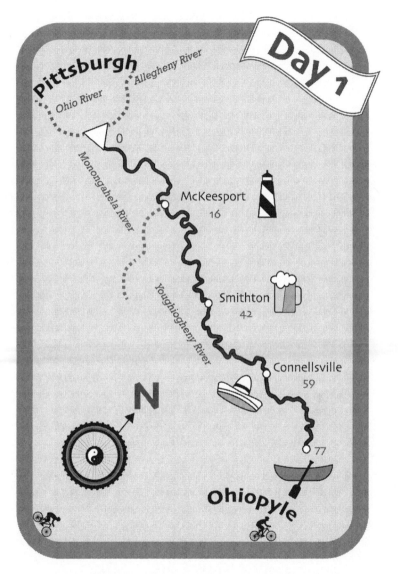

Point State Park, Pittsburgh, Pa to Ohiopyle, Pa

10

MCKEESPORT

arty and I started out at an easy pace. It was rush hour, and as we rode along Pittsburgh's Southside we could hear the sounds of traffic and honking horns. As we passed under the Birmingham Bridge, we looked up and saw cars whizzing by overhead. Normally I too would have been driving to work at this time on a Monday, thinking about all I had to get done during the week. But today I was enjoying the beautiful morning on my bike.

As this was August, Marty was already two months into his summer "chill mode," his daily teaching duties the furthest thing from his mind. But he also noticed the traffic.

"Jimbo, you know how I get home around 2:30 p.m. every day during the school year?" Marty asked.

"Yeah, I know," I said jealously. We were riding side-by-side as no one else was on the trail.

"Well, I typically take a nap, and then I ride my bike for a couple of hours."

"Right," I said. *In my next life I will be Marty.*

"Okay, so, as I wrap up my ride around 5:00 p.m., I

usually ride alongside that highway over there." Marty pointed across the river at I-376, known as "the Parkway," the main thoroughfare running through Pittsburgh. "I see the same thing we're seeing now. You would not believe the amount of traffic out here at that time. It's asphyxiating breathing all that exhaust."

"Yes Marty, that's called *rush hour*," I said. "Much of the rest of the world is on the road at that time because they need to work until at least 5:00 p.m."

Marty laughed and shook his head. "Yeah, Jimbo, I guess that's it."

The trail took us past the Southside Works, where Marty and I had enjoyed our beers at the Hofbrauhaus a few months earlier. The "Works" is an outdoor shopping complex on the site of the former Jones & Laughlin (J&L) Steel Mill which ran continuously from 1854 to 1983. The J&L used to produce so much smoke and ash that Pittsburgh was referred to as "Hell with The Lid Off," and street lamps burned all day long to compensate for the darkened skies. We rode under the Hot Metal Bridge, a bridge that the J&L used to transport molten steel in metal containers from one side of the river to the other.

Next we passed the Carrie Furnace, an enormous blast furnace which was originally part of Homestead Steel Works, now preserved as a National Historic Landmark. I reflected that the industry that once employed the majority of Pittsburghers is now becoming a distant memory.

As we rode through Homestead, we passed Kennywood, Pittsburgh's iconic amusement park which first opened in 1899 and still attracts over one million visitors each year. Across the Monongahela we saw Turtle Creek, the site where General Braddock and his men were crushed by the French in 1755. The town now bears his name.

After a few more miles, we arrived in McKeesport, where the Youghiogheny River flows into the Monongahela.

~

In the mid-1700s, this confluence was the home of a band of Seneca Indians headed by Queen Aliquippa. George Washington came here to visit the Queen on his first trip to western Pennsylvania in 1753. She and her Seneca group then became a key ally of the British during the buildup to the French and Indian War.

In 1795, John McKee, an original settler of Philadelphia, built a log cabin here and established a river ferry business. He then formed a city and called it McKee's Port.

The city began to grow in the 1830s when coal mining started, and McKeesport's first steel mill was built in 1851. The National Tube Company opened in McKeesport in 1872 and eventually became one of the world's largest manufacturers of welded steel tubes, used for water and gas mains, refinery piping and many other applications.

Over the next twenty years, McKeesport was the fastest growing municipality in the nation. Families arrived from other parts of the eastern United States, as well as from Germany, Italy, Poland, Russia, Czechoslovakia and Hungary to work at National Tube. By 1940, the city's population was over 55,000.

~

As with many cities in western Pennsylvania, the decline of the steel industry hit McKeesport hard. Now, the population of McKeesport is less than 20,000 and the city suffers from high unemployment and crime.

But Riverfront Park, at the confluence of the two rivers, is a beautiful and peaceful spot. And right there, at the start of the bike trail, we were stunned at what we saw – a twenty-foot high exact replica of the lighthouse in Cape Hatteras. It was incredible – every detail matched the actual lighthouse we had visited each summer for the last eight years. We decided this was a very good sign and meant that we would have a successful trip.

Replica of Cape Hatteras Lighthouse - McKeesport, PA

From the intersection of the "Yough" and the "Mon," the GAP trail heads up the Yough, with the river on the left. By now it was approaching eighty degrees with low humidity – perfect biking weather. We passed a waterfall running down the side of a rock wall which had turned orange from the high iron levels in the water. Then we passed Versailles, PA, a quaint village along the Yough. Unlike the French, the locals here pronounce it exactly as spelled: "Ver-saylz."

An important thing to know about Marty is that when he rides, he never likes to be passed by another rider. Like a teenage male driver, he takes it as a personal challenge when someone passes him, and he accelerates until he catches up. Then he typically engages the person in conversation as he is always interested in talking to other serious riders.

Just past Versailles, as Marty and I were riding along comfortably, suddenly we heard a voice from behind us: *"Passing on your left!"* I pulled in single file behind Marty and a man in his thirties blazed past us.

Marty took off after him. Like a dog chasing a car, he immediately forgot about me and focused on his mission. He needed to catch that biker. I maintained my easy pace and let him go.

After about thirty minutes, I saw Marty on the side of the trail waiting for me. I approached and he again pulled in alongside of me.

"Did you catch him?" I asked.

"Yup. He's from Pittsburgh, just going to Ohiopyle today," Marty replied.

"Good guy?"

"Yeah. I rode with him for a bit. It was funny – he asked me 'Hey, does your friend mind that you ride way ahead of him like this?'" Marty recounted.

"What did you tell him?"

"I said, 'That guy? That's Jimbo. He rides at his own pace.'"

He was right. For the next five days, I would keep my

consistent pace at about twelve miles an hour, while Marty established a pattern of riding along with me for a couple of hours, then accelerating to chase passing bikers, followed by long stretches sitting on the side of the trail waiting for me to catch up. Marty got his enhanced cardio workout and had time to sit, while I had time to myself to think. And we had many hours together for inane conversation.

Day 1 on the trail – near Versailles, PA

11

THE BREWERY

As we rode along the trail that first day, we saw a sign indicating the mileage to several upcoming towns. One of those towns was Smithton, a borough which Marty and I had visited many times in the past and which held a significant place in the history of our friendship.

∼

In 1986, Marty and I had agreed we would have a "cultural exchange" of local beers during one of their summer visits from Pittsburgh to Maryland. Marty brought a case of Stoney's, a working-class beer made in Smithton. As my end of the bargain, I presented a case of National Bohemian, a Baltimore-based blue-collar beer with the nickname "Natty-Bo." We spent the weekend sipping the beers and swapping stories about local cultures.

Katie and I then moved to Northern California in 1988 where I attended graduate school and worked in Silicon Valley. One summer, we agreed to meet Belle and Marty for a camping trip in the Grand Canyon. Katie and I drove across the Mojave desert; Belle and Marty drove five days across the country from Pittsburgh. We met at the edge of the Canyon.

Once the tents were up, Marty presented the prize he'd transported for over 2,000 miles – a case of Stoney's beer. In fact, when he told the beer distributor in Pittsburgh that he was taking the Stoney's out to Arizona, the salesman said, "That'll be a strange beast out there."

Well it *was* a strange beast. The case was a plain brown cardboard box with the Stoney's logo in red ink on the outside. The box also stated that inside we would find twenty-four sixteen-ounce bottles – each one labeled "The Pounder." We eagerly opened the case and soon noticed that all the labels were upside-down. I suppose this made them easier to read when looking at them from above.

Without any ice at the campsite, we drank the beers warm. Katie and I shared stories of our new life in California, while Belle and Marty updated us on what was happening back home.

Vintage can of Stoney's Beer

Katie and I eventually moved back to Maryland in 1991.

While visiting her family in Pittsburgh that Thanksgiving, Marty and I decided we'd make a pilgrimage to the Stoney's brewery the next day to visit the source of the infamous beer. We managed to convince a few other guys to go with us, probably just so they could avoid accompanying their wives to the mall on Black Friday. We all donned flannel shirts as it was a cold, gray day.

The Stoney's brewmaster gave us a tour of the brewery, followed by an invitation to the "Hospitality Tap Room." Over the next two hours, we sampled all the beers brewed by the Stoney's brewery, including Penn Pilsner, a barley wine, and many others. Monitoring the proceedings from his portrait on the wall was Stoney Jones, the barrel-chested man who founded the brewery in 1906.

Portrait of Stoney Jones in the Hospitality Tap Room

Marty is always interested in people and in history, so he engaged the brewmaster in conversation. It turned out that the brewmaster himself was descended from "the old man" Stoney Jones. Also, we learned that Shirley Jones, the actress and singer made famous by *The Partridge Family* and *The Music Man*, was the grand-daughter of Stoney Jones and the pride of Smithton.

We left the brewery and went to the Longhorn Saloon, the main bar in town. It took a few seconds for our eyes to adjust to the darkness inside. The room was filled with smoke, but through the cloudy air we could make out several men playing pool on the far end of the room, as well as about a dozen others sitting around the bar. Everyone stopped what they were doing and focused on us as we slowly stepped into the bar. The place went silent.

Marty walked over to the bar and started speaking to the bartender. I couldn't make out what they were saying. The bartender nodded. Then he cupped his hand to his mouth and said in a raised voice, "Hey everyone, Marty here is buying everyone a round!"

The place erupted in a cheer as the men pounded the bar – to a chorus of "*Marty... Marty... Marty...*" And as the bartender busily worked to fill orders – all for Stoney's beer of course – they crowded around Marty, shook his hand and engaged in conversation. After the crowd cleared, I grabbed a stool next to Marty.

"Marty, that was genius," I said.

"Yeah, it was fun talking to these guys and getting a little local flavor," said Marty.

"What did that cost you to buy that round?" I asked.

"Eight bucks. Stoney's drafts were fifty cents each," Marty said.

Marty and I spotted a massive moose head on the far wall, with Christmas decorations on both sides. We walked over to it and had one of the guys take a picture of us, both indicating a one-handed "thumbs up."

For the next nine years, Marty and I led a group to Smithton and the Stoney's brewery the day after Thanksgiving. It was a great tradition, and our group grew to as many as twenty guys. Marty and I continued to take a picture under the moose head each year, and each year we held up our hands indicating the number of years we'd been there.

Marty and Jim under the moose head in 1994 (year 4)

Unfortunately, we never had to go beyond displaying all of our fingers on both hands. Our tradition ultimately ended on the tenth anniversary when the brewery ownership changed hands. At that point we decided to find a new tradition.

12

SMITHTON

A fter another hour on the trail, and now forty-two miles into our first day, we arrived in Smithton. We hadn't been there in ten years. We also had never seen Smithton when it wasn't cloaked in November's gray skies, and we had never approached it from the river. We decided to get off the trail, see the town again and meet some locals.

The Stoney's brewery had employed most of the town for nearly a century. On our annual visit, the workers would tell us about their fathers and grandfathers who had worked in the brewery. They said that during their lunch breaks, they would be handed a tin bucket with several Stoney's beers to consume before they returned for their afternoon shift.

We were shocked at what Smithton had become. After running continuously since 1906, the brewery finally shut down operations in 2001. We rode our bikes over to the "House of Jones" – it was locked up with CLOSED signs on the doors. Looking up, we saw sumac trees growing out of the roof. We got off our bikes and walked around the building. We peered in the windows and saw the office – it was as if it were frozen in time; a calendar hung on the wall, pens and pencils still lay on the desk, and Stoney's signs were on the walls, everywhere. It looked the same as when we were there many years ago.

We biked over to the Longhorn Saloon, where Marty had bought the men a round of beer every year. Surely that was still open and serving beers to some local residents? Sadly, our favorite Smithton watering hole was also boarded up and permanently closed.

As we were getting ready to leave town, we saw a tent canopy set up with volunteer firemen selling hoagies out of a cooler chest as a fundraiser. They spoke of the closing of the brewery and the hard times the town had fallen on since then.

As Marty and I pulled out of town and got back on the trail, we reflected on how good things don't last forever. We had a lot of miles ahead of us that day, so we put Smithton behind us and fell into the cycling rhythm again.

13

THE PLAYER

As we rode along, I began to settle into the mode of simply taking in the scenery, breathing the sweet summer air, and letting my mind wander.

We passed several small river towns – Whitsett, Layton, then Dawson. The Yough river on the left was peaceful, flat and wide. We passed modest homes on the right, and occasionally we would see kids playing in their yards. At one point, we passed four teenage boys playing a two-on-two basketball game. It reminded me of the days when Marty and I used to shoot hoops together.

~

During the 1990s, before we moved to Pittsburgh, Katie and I lived on a cul-de-sac in Olney, Maryland, a typical suburban neighborhood where we raised our three sons.

A friend of mine from work, John, lived nearby in Rockville. He and his wife, Sylvia, had two children, and Sylvia and Katie were good friends. We would hang out with

John and Sylvia often, having cookouts at each other's houses and watching each other's kids.

One Friday in July, I saw John at work and we were talking about the weekend. John had been out of town all week, and it had been a long week for me as well.

"What are you up to this weekend?" asked John.

"Katie's sister, Belle, and her family are coming into town from Pittsburgh."

"Sounds fun. I don't think Sylvia and I have ever met them. You all want to come over to our house for a swim in our pool?"

"Sounds great. We'll bring some snacks and a dessert."

Belle and Marty arrived that evening, and Marty brought his road bike. On Saturday morning, he asked me if I wanted to go for a ride with him, but I told him I didn't have a bike. He asked if I knew anyone who might have a bike I could borrow. After calling a few neighbors, I was able to borrow one – a high end carbon-fiber road bike. I had never ridden such a thing. We adjusted the seat and it seemed like it would work out well.

Marty and I took off on our bikes and were soon on the back-country winding roads of Northern Montgomery County, Maryland. It was hot, but moving along at fifteen miles an hour created a nice breeze which cooled us off. We passed by a patch of honeysuckle and breathed in the sweet scent. We cruised through wooded areas, cow pastures, corn fields, and eventually made our way back to the house. Marty got ahead of me for the second half of the trip, and by the end I was exhausted. We had ridden about twenty-five miles.

"How'd you like that, Jimbo?"

"It was great, but I'm wiped out and you haven't even broken a sweat." I was still panting.

"Yeah, look at you. The sweat is dripping off your nose like a faucet. Drip, drip, drip..." Marty got a kick out of how much water was coming out of my body.

Around noon, we all headed over to John and Sylvia's house. Belle and Marty got a chance to chat with our friends during the course of the afternoon. John had a basketball hoop in his driveway and asked Marty and me if we'd like to play two-on-two with him and his son.

We played hard for about an hour. Afterwards we took another dip in the pool before heading back to our house. After popping open a couple of beers, Marty took me aside.

"Jimbo, how well do you know John?"

"Really well, why?"

"*Really* well?"

"Yeah," I said. "I work with him. Our families hang out all the time, do cookouts together, that kind of stuff. Why?"

"Well, Jimbo, I don't know how to tell you this..."

"What?"

"Jimbo, he's a player."

"Yeah, I know, he's pretty good," I said. "I think he played basketball in high school."

"No, I mean he's a *player*."

"What? What do you mean?" I was confused.

Marty sighed and looked at me with an unusually serious expression. "He's cheating on his wife."

"What??" I thought this was one of Marty's jokes. But he wasn't laughing. "What makes you think that?"

"I can tell by the way he plays basketball."

"How can you tell that from basketball?" I was totally puzzled by this.

"It's obvious," Marty shrugged. "His moves on the court. He's a player."

I changed the subject and then forgot about the conversation. Katie and I continued to hang out with John and Sylvia, having a lot of fun together.

Four months later, Sylvia told Katie that she and John were getting a divorce. John had been cheating on her for over a year. I was stunned. Marty had been right. I called Marty and told him.

"*How did you know*?" I asked him.

"It was obvious."

"*What* was obvious?"

"The way he played basketball," said Marty. "The more amazing thing is that you *didn't* notice it."

"What else can you detect playing basketball? Can you tell if I have cancer if we play a little one-on-one?" I asked.

"Don't be silly Jimbo, it only works for certain things. Like personality traits."

~

I never really got a satisfactory answer from Marty as to what specifically he saw in John's moves that led him to be so confident in diagnosing his infidelity. But through this experience I realized that Marty is a very observant person and tunes into things that many other people miss.

As we biked along the GAP trail on that first day, I brought up the story again. Marty laughed as he recalled that day.

"Marty, how *did* you know that guy was a player?"

"Players have something they are hiding – a secret," said Marty. "I could tell by the way he played basketball that he was hiding something."

YES, MY FRIEND

Around 1:00 p.m. we had been riding for over five hours and nearly sixty miles – we were ready to eat. We were approaching the town of Connellsville. It was here that General Braddock and his men crossed the Youghiogheny on their ill-fated march toward Fort Duquesne in 1755.

Connellsville also played an important role in the steel industry, as it was located in the center of the Connellsville Coalfield, where coal mining boomed during the late nineteenth and early twentieth centuries. Connellsville was known for making coke, a purified form of coal with high carbon content. Coke burned at the high temperatures needed to fire an iron furnace used to make steel.

Connellsville was known as the "Coke Capital of the World." Coke ovens (known as "beehive ovens" because of their shape) were built into the hillsides along the Youghiogheny River. The railroad transported the coke from Connellsville down the Yough to McKeesport, and then down the Monongahela to the steel mills in Pittsburgh.

Coke made Connellsville wealthy. The town boasted

beautiful Victorian homes, banks, and many restaurants and shops. Life was good while the steel industry thrived.

Today, Connellsville has a population of only 7,000 and is largely a trail town. As Marty and I got closer, we spotted some of the abandoned beehive coke ovens on our right and imagined workers pulling out the coke and shoveling it onto the train cars which once occupied the GAP.

We got off the trail and looked for a place to eat. As we rode through town, we passed a beautiful old bank which had been boarded up, followed by one Victorian house after another in disrepair. Clearly this had been a great town in its day, but not this day.

Finally we found one restaurant which was open – a Mexican place called El Canelo. We were a bit hesitant to eat Mexican food in the middle of the day, with eighteen miles of riding still ahead of us. But without any other options, we decided this was it.

We were very dirty as we had hit a few patches of mud on the trail. We stood outside the restaurant's window, got our bikes situated and tried to brush off some of the grime. Just inside the window, the restaurant's proprietor, a tall man with jet-black hair, stood wrapping silverware in napkins. We watched him for a minute, yet he never looked up at us. Although we made quite a commotion outside, he continued with his task as if he was hoping we would go away.

Of course, we didn't. We entered the place, still muddy and with our bike shoes on. He offered us a table. We sat down, glad to feel the air conditioning and to have a glass of ice water in front of us.

We opened the menus (remember, biking makes you hungry), and were presented with the typical array of Mexican food offerings, all of which combine the same essential six ingredients in different ways – beans, rice, cheese, chicken, beef and a tortilla shell. My high school math helped me calculate that these six ingredients could create 720 different combinations – and about 700 of them were offered on this menu.

Overwhelmed by the choices, we looked at the first thing on the menu. Top left – the #1 lunch special – the Speedy Gonzales. One taco, one enchilada, and a choice of rice or beans, for $5.95. The restaurant's owner was also our waiter. When he arrived at our table, we asked him whether the Speedy Gonzales would be a good choice. He responded with a simple "Yes, my friend." The decision was made – we ordered two of them.

After we placed our orders, Marty got up and headed to the men's room to clean up a little. I began munching on chips and salsa and looked around the room. There were only two other occupied tables – one by a couple at the far end, and one by a middle-aged woman sitting alone in the booth directly across from us. I made brief eye contact with her and nodded, then focused again on the chips.

Suddenly, she broke the silence.

"Vaht ah you doing?" she asked me in a strange accent.

Connellsville is an isolated town in the middle of Fayette County, Pennsylvania, where the only accent you typically hear is "Pittsburghese," an endearing dialect with terms like "yinz" and "n'at."

"You ah all messy – vaht ah you doing?" she asked again. Her accent sounded French to me. Or maybe Eastern European.

"Riding our bikes to Washington, DC," I answered.

"Vashington?! Vhere did you staht?" I was trying hard to place that accent.

"Pittsburgh."

"How long vill dat take?" she asked.

"We're doing it in five days." My curiosity got the best of me. "Excuse me, but I'm trying to place your accent – and I'm guessing you're not from Connellsville. Where are you from?"

"I am indeed from Connellsville," she answered. "And you von't be able to place my accent, because I have... foreign accent syndrome!"

Just then, Marty returned from the men's room and rejoined me at our table. I motioned to him and tilted my head toward the lady across from me. I said under my breath, *"Marty, you gotta get in on this."*

I took the bait. "What is foreign accent syndrome?" I asked her.

"Vell, about zeven years ago, I had a stroke. I vas in a coma for several veeks, and vhen I voke up, my voice zounded like dis!"

"Huh?" Marty's eyes opened wide.

"Yah, zum days it zounds French, udder days Russian. Only about zeventy people in the vorld have it – it is very unusual. In fact I vas on the Today Show – dey did a story about it and about me."

"Well, I have never heard of such a thing," I said. She seemed very happy to have a newcomer to talk to, as it was likely that everyone in Connellsville already knew about her rare condition.

"You know you ah crazy to ride your bikes all dat vay," she said.

"Yes, but it is a challenge and we are excited about it," I responded.

She shook her head, muttering "Boys vill be boys..." to herself as she went back to eating her lunch.

We were still processing this odd encounter as our

Speedy Gonzales's arrived. Fast, like the name. We plowed down the food. Marty always craved a Diet Coke while riding, so we ordered two of them. "Yes, my friend" was the reply, and soon two ice-cold Diet Cokes were in front of us.

"Did you notice that this guy always says 'Yes, my friend' every time we ask him something?" Marty pointed out.

"Yeah, it's really polite, but kind of odd that he does it every time," I said.

"Well, let's see how many more times we can get him to say it," Marty suggested with a grin, appealing to my adolescent sense of humor.

"Great idea."

The next time he passed by, I asked for some more water. *"Yes, my friend."*

Then more chips. *"Yes, my friend."*

Then more salsa. *"Yes, my friend."*

When we were satisfied, we asked for the bill. Naturally, we got a *"Yes, my friend."* We paid, got back on our bikes, and started making our way through town back to the trail, our bellies full of spicy, heavy, Mexican food.

15

THE PARKING JOB

W e got back on the trail and headed east toward Ohiopyle. The eighty-seven mile section of the GAP between Connellsville and Cumberland was originally occupied by the Western Maryland Railroad. Once the railroad was no longer in use, the Western Pennsylvania Conservancy worked to convert it to the initial section of the GAP trail, which opened in 1986.

The GAP trail to the east of Connellsville is peaceful and beautiful, with the Yough river making one sweeping bend after another. Marty outpaced me, and I rode alone for a while. Again my mind started wandering. I remembered another trip Belle and Marty had made to visit us in Maryland during another summer, a couple of years after the experience with the Player.

~

That weekend, we had decided to take all the boys into Washington, DC to see some of the sights. We took two cars and worked our way from our house in Olney down Georgia

Avenue into the city. At one point, Marty was in front of me and I noticed that his car was filthy. Clearly he had not washed it in months. I could barely see him through the thick film of dirt on his back window.

We arrived in DC and circled around the Mall for a while looking for parking spaces. It was a Saturday in July and the city was packed with tourists. We split up and eventually were successful – Marty parked near the Air and Space Museum and I left my car near the Washington Monument. We all converged at the Air and Space, toured the museum with the boys, and then threw the Frisbee around outside for a while. It was a wonderful afternoon.

Dinnertime was approaching and we were getting hungry, so we rounded up the boys and headed for the cars. Marty's car was nearby and we walked over together. As we passed the front, I noticed his car was very close to the car in front of him – their bumpers separated by only a few inches.

As we rounded the back of his car, Marty suddenly stopped. The rest of us looked up – everyone saw it at the same time and we all stopped in our tracks. We were speechless as we stared at his back window in horror.

There, written by someone using their finger in the dirt on Marty's rear window, was a message in capital letters:

YOU PARK LIKE AN ASSHOLE

Marty was paralyzed.

I tugged on his arm. "Marty, it's no big deal, we can wash it off when we get back to our house."

He had lost the power of speech and couldn't pull himself away. He read the message over and over and at one point hung his head and sighed.

Belle eventually shook Marty out of his trance and got

him into the car. Katie, the boys, and I walked over to our car and we all drove back to our house. When we arrived, we got out the hose and washed off Marty's back window.

We cooked burgers on the grill that night. Afterwards, sitting on our deck outside, Marty brought it up again.

"Jimbo, that message is really bothering me."

Marty was taking this personally, and I had the feeling that he might stew on it for weeks. I had to come up with something to get it off his mind.

"Do *you* think I'm an asshole, Jimbo?" Marty asked.

I thought some more.

"Marty, think about how that message is worded: 'You *park like* an asshole.' That person wasn't saying you *are* an asshole," I said.

"What?" Marty seemed interested. I had his attention.

"Not even close," I continued. "The message is essentially: '*If* you were an asshole, this is how you would park.' Or, more accurately, 'If *one* were an asshole, this is how one *might* park.'" I was trying to appeal to Marty's sense of reason.

"Huh. That *is* a bit different."

"Think about it, Marty. If they wanted to say you were an asshole, they would have just written something like 'Nice parking job, asshole!' It's completely different."

"Yeah!" said Marty. I could see his energy returning. "Or maybe 'Hey asshole, move your car!' You're right, Jimbo, I do feel better. Thanks for clarifying it."

We all went to bed and Marty didn't bring it up the next day. But he was a bit quieter than normal and I knew it was still affecting him. From this experience I realized that, despite Marty's tough exterior and street-wise personality, he is a very sensitive person and sometimes it takes him a while to process things.

16

OHIOPYLE

Back on the trail, about ten miles past Connellsville, the Yough begins to narrow and the current moves faster. The flat, calm surface begins to churn white as rocks break through the surface. On the right are trees, rock walls, and an occasional clearing with a few houses.

As we moved along, the sound of the river grew stronger. We heard the rushing of whitewater as the torrent forced its way past large boulders. The trail followed the snaking path the river had cut, and we made several sharp bends.

With a little over a mile to Ohiopyle, we crossed a high bridge which was used by the railroad years before. We stopped and looked down at the river below. We could hear the rapids from our high perch and watched as two kayakers skillfully picked their way through the rock course.

We got back on our bikes and soon crossed another bridge which led us into Ohiopyle, the centerpiece of the Yough river. On weekends in the summertime, the town is a bustling place - full of whitewater rafters, hikers and bikers. Since Ohiopyle is set in a valley, the air is often filled with the scent of burning brake pads.

On a Monday evening, the town is largely empty. We found the Ohiopyle Lodge, hosed our bikes down, then showered and changed. One day and seventy-seven miles behind us – only 258 miles to go!

Jim arriving in Ohiopyle, PA (note image of Stoney's bottle on right)

We bought a six pack at Fall's Market and headed down to the river. Ohiopyle comes from the Native American word "Ohiopehelle" which means "white, frothy water." There is a twenty-foot waterfall in the middle of town – an awesome, constant reminder of the power of the river.

In 1754, George Washington arrived here, hoping to travel by boat the rest of the way to the Forks of the Ohio. However, upon seeing these intimidating falls and the rapids below, he decided to take a land route, which led to him running into and firing on the French and Indians a few miles west of here, starting the Seven Years' War.

Upstream of Ohiopyle is a six-mile calm stretch of river where people take lazy float and fishing trips. Downstream is an eight mile whitewater course with Class 3 and 4 rapids – the section we had just traversed on our bikes. Marty and I and our families have done both rafting trips many times.

Waterfall in Ohiopyle, PA

Marty and I sat and drank our beers, taking in the sunset and listening to the thunder of the waterfall. Then we walked around town, past familiar places such as Laurel Highlands River Tours and Wilderness Voyageurs, where we'd rented rafts in our younger days. We found an outdoor table at the Ohiopyle House Café, got some dinner and then headed back to our room. Sleep came easily after waking up early and spending all day on our bikes.

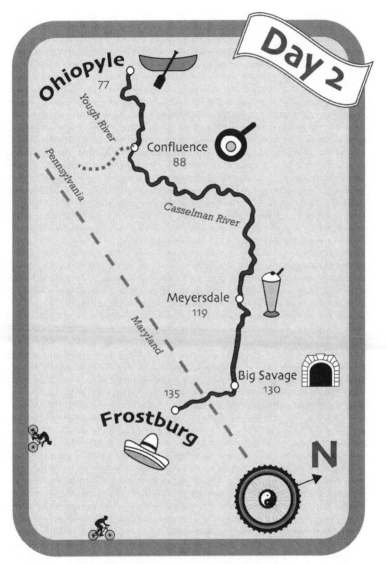

Day 2

Ohiopyle 77

Yough River

Pennsylvania

Confluence 88

Casselman River

Maryland

Meyersdale 119

Big Savage 130

135

Frostburg

N

Ohiopyle, Pa to Frostburg, Md

17

HAPPY BIRTHDAY

I woke up before Marty the next morning and made a pot of coffee in our room. The soreness in my butt and legs were an immediate reminder of the long ride the day before. I filled my cup, then stepped outside and headed down to the river to catch another glimpse of the waterfall in the dawn's emerging light.

Two squirrels were running back and forth across the grass in front of me. As I approached, they scurried up a tree. I found a spot under the tree with a perfect view of the falls. As I sipped my coffee, I chuckled to myself as I recalled some of Marty's run-ins with squirrels over the last few months.

≈

As far as I know, Marty has only two physical frailties. One of them is his eyesight, as he is both near and far-sighted. He has a dozen pairs of reading glasses around the house and in his car, but he can never seem to find one when he needs it. And to my knowledge he doesn't own a pair of regular glasses to help him see things at a distance. This combination can sometimes cause problems.

One day in July, about a month before the bike trip, I had been texting Marty with some questions about what to bring. At one point in our text conversation he texted a *Happy Birthday* graphic complete with animated balloons flying across the screen. As my birthday is in May, I thought this was odd, not to mention that it made no sense in the context of our conversation. I soon forgot about it.

That Saturday, Katie and I went over to Belle and Marty's for dinner and were sitting on the front porch. Traffic was buzzing by with the occasional siren in the distance.

"Hey, Jumbo, you good to go for this trip?" Marty asked me.

"I think so," I replied. I turned my head toward him. "Did you just call me *Jumbo*?"

Marty chuckled. "Yeah. I have that name stuck in my mind. Jumbo!"

"Why, might I ask?"

"Well, you know how I can't see without my glasses? And how I can never find a pair? Well, when I typed your name into my contacts on my cell phone, I was trying to type 'Jimbo' and accidentally typed a 'u' instead of an 'i.' My phone is paired with my car, so when I'm driving, every time you call me, my dashboard reads, *Call from... Jumbo*. It kind of stuck in my mind."

"Not sure how I feel about it..." At 5'8" and relatively slim, it didn't seem to fit.

Marty was laughing heartily. "So, Jumbo, you ready for a burger tonight?"

I began to resign myself to the new nickname.

As I sat on the porch, I spotted something I had never

seen before. A rifle was leaning up against the wall in the corner.

"Is that... a rifle? Why do you have a rifle, Marty?" I asked.

"It's not a rifle. It is a Squirrel Eradication Device," Marty replied.

He continued, "We have squirrels all over the roof of our house. They've been chewing through the eaves for years. I could set traps, but I'd have to find a way to get up there. So instead I shoot them."

"What does that thing shoot?"

"It's an air gun – it shoots pellets. But it's enough to kill them."

"You do that right here in the middle of the city?" I asked.

"Yeah, but I try to do it when the family isn't around, like when they're at church. I tend to have good luck on high holidays – I got a big one on Easter Sunday."

Marty proceeded to tell me about how many squirrels he has "eradicated" and how he disposes of them in the garbage afterwards – double wrapped in Ziploc bags with paper towel, "like a hoagie," he said.

"Last Sunday I was out here and I heard one in the eaves up there." Marty pointed to the front corner of the house. "I got out the gun... I mean eradication device... and pointed it up at him. And you know how I can't see and can never find my glasses?"

"Yeah," I replied.

"Well, I pulled the trigger and down in front of me falls... a bluejay," Marty said laughing.

"Bluejays do look a lot like squirrels – *if you're blind*!" I said.

As we waited for Belle to finish making dinner, Marty

asked me, "Hey Jumbo, did I by any chance text you *Happy Birthday* a couple of days ago?"

"Yes you did."

"Well, with my bad eyes, I think I hit the wrong key and sent that greeting by mistake. I saw it later, once I put my glasses on. Sorry about that."

Marty continued, "Hey, I gotta tell you about something else that happened this week that has to do with the same thing. You know Chris, the guy I go mountain biking with sometimes?"

"Yeah."

"Chris and I were biking at Frick Park two nights ago," Marty explained. "It's pretty technical and challenging in there, but Chris is a great rider. We have a typical route we take in the park, and he was a bit behind me. I finished up and rode to the parking lot. I got the chairs set up and had the beers ready."

"Uh-huh."

"I was sitting there for ten or fifteen minutes and no sign of Chris. I got a text which I thought might be from him, but since I didn't have my glasses I couldn't tell what it said. I hit a reply but was pretty sure I messed up the message."

"Yeah, then what?"

"I got on my bike and went back into the woods to look for him, but couldn't find him. I kept yelling his name – nothing. And it was dark by then. I was getting a little worried."

"Yikes."

"So I rode back to my car and opened a beer and waited. After another fifteen minutes, I heard something rustling in the woods. Out comes Chris on his hands and knees, dragging himself along the ground."

"Jeez!"

"I ran over to him and asked him what had happened. He said he had a bad crash, flew over the handlebars and landed on the ground. The wind was knocked out of him and he thought he may have broken a rib or even punctured a lung. He said I was pretty close when I went back looking for him and he heard me yelling his name – he tried yelling back but his voice was too faint from the injuries. He told me he texted me."

"So that text *was* from Chris?"

"Yeah, and after I got him into my car and we were on our way to the hospital, I found my reading glasses and looked at the text."

"What did it say?"

"It said, *Crashed. Hurt. Bad. Need help.*"

"And what was your response?"

Marty hung his head sheepishly. "I texted *Happy Birthday*. Chris told me once he saw the balloons, he knew it was up to him to save himself."

Chris was treated for his injuries and was okay. But Marty still doesn't bother much with reading glasses.

18

THE O'HENRY

Back in Ohiopyle, I finished my coffee, pulled myself away from the mesmerizing view of the falls and headed back to our room. Marty was awake and finishing his coffee.

"Jimbo, did you already take care of business?" I knew exactly what he meant.

"Yeah, I did that as soon as I woke up. Like clockwork," I answered.

"Show-off," said Marty.

Marty's other physical frailty is that he finds it difficult to stay regular outside of a thirty mile radius of his home.

"Sorry, Marty, maybe you'll have better luck tomorrow."

"Yeah, maybe. Well, anyway, time to get up and ride!" he said.

We did exactly that. Marty suggested we start the day by riding the first eleven miles to Confluence, stopping for breakfast at a diner called Sisters Café. The stretch from Ohiopyle to Confluence was the very first section of the GAP to be completed – in 1986 – and it is beautiful. It's an easy, flat ride under a canopy of trees, with the Yough on the left and an occasional train on the other side of the river. We arrived in Confluence in less than an hour, rode into town and found the Sisters Café. It wasn't crowded, and the waitress seated us at a booth and brought us menus.

"Jimbo, I didn't bring my reading glasses, what does this say?" asked Marty, pointing at something on the menu.

I began reading the menu to Marty (yes, although I don't read books, I do read menus). At one point, the waitress came to our table, pulled out her pad and pen and watched as I read each item. Marty wanted to hear all the descriptions, so it was taking a while.

"Jimbo, what's in that western omelet again?"

"Ham, cheese, green peppers..."

"Yinz guys ready to order?" interrupted the waitress.

I had only made it as far as the omelets, and Marty wanted to hear the rest of the menu.

"Can you give us another minute?" I asked.

"No problem." She walked away and began serving another table.

I read the rest of the menu, and when she returned, we were ready to order. We had ham and cheese omelets, hash browns, bacon and toast. A nice light meal to get our burners going.

We got up and went over to the counter to pay the bill. At the counter there were candy bars for sale. Marty spotted the O'Henry's, bought two of them and gave one to me. "Tuck that in your bag, Jimbo. It'll be a nice snack later on."

"Marty, I always thought we'd be eating power bars and bananas and drinking Gatorade. Instead we're eating candy bars and heavy food, and drinking Diet Cokes."

"That's right, Jimbo."

We got on our bikes and headed southeast on the GAP trail. Confluence is a very descriptive name, because the town is literally the confluence of the Yough and the Casselman River. We left the Yough and picked up the Casselman, an equally beautiful river with frequent riffles.

We passed through a few small towns, the largest of which was Rockwood, with a population of 954 and median household income of $25,000. Having spent my life in relatively affluent areas, it was eye-opening to see how modestly much of America lives.

Bridge over the Casselman River, near Rockwood, PA

Recall that Ohiopyle is at 1200 feet elevation and Confluence is at 1330 feet. During the course of Day 2, we would climb to 2400 feet at the top of Big Savage Mountain and ride a total of fifty-eight miles. It was hot and sections of the trail were exposed to the sun. I was really thirsty.

Marty had said that later this day we would pass the town of Meyersdale, where he'd had an incredible milkshake when he rode this section of the trail a few years earlier. As we droned along, my mind became focused on the milkshake. I refrained from talking about it, keeping to the ten-mile rule. But I was thinking about it. I had looked at a map and had located Meyersdale, so I had a good idea of how far we had to go. Marty of course never bothers with maps (recall: *"Get up and ride"*).

Marty got ahead of me, and I was riding on my own for about an hour and a half. I didn't see or pass anyone – I was all alone. The thoughts of the milkshake were getting stronger. Would I get vanilla? Chocolate with malt? Or something else? Whipped cream? Cherry or no cherry?

Just then, in the distance, I saw a figure sitting on a bench. I surmised it was Marty, and as I drew closer, I saw him sitting there, looking despondent. He was eating his O'Henry bar.

"We must have missed it, Jimbo."

"Missed what?" I asked.

"Meyersdale. We passed it," Marty said as he chomped on the candy bar.

"I don't think so," I insisted. "I looked at the map, and I think we have a couple of miles to go. *Why are you eating your O' Henry bar?! I thought we were getting milkshakes!*"

"Well, I'm sure we passed it. So the O'Henry is gonna have to do."

I refused to accept this. I had just spent the last two hours thinking about a milkshake – in detail – and at that point I *needed* a milkshake.

"Let's go, Marty." I could not get him off the bench. He was a beaten man.

While I waited for him, I stormed around, trying to hold back my frustration. The bench was facing a beautiful vista – green hills in the distance with meadows of wildflowers in front of us and a red barn on top of a hill. I stomped across the bike trail to the other side and discovered several headstones in a patch of tall grass. I walked further into the grass and found twenty or thirty more headstones – a cemetery! A number of them were from the late 1800s and early 1900s – and the last name on every headstone was *Meyers.*

I leapt out of the tall grass and ran back across the trail to where Marty was still sitting on the bench.

"Marty, we're close!"

"Close to what?" he asked, somewhat disinterested.

"Meyersdale! I found the Meyers' cemetery – across the trail there. They're are all buried there. We gotta be close!"

Marty slowly got up off the bench to check it out for himself. He came back, clapped his hands, pumped his fists in the air and said, "I guess I was wrong! Let's go, Jimbo!"

We got on our bikes and immediately crossed a large bridge (the Salisbury Viaduct, hereafter known as the "Bridge to Happiness"). From the middle of the bridge we looked down and to the right and saw the town. There it was! Meyersdale!

Meyersdale sits below the bike trail. We got off the trail and descended into town. We quickly came to the Pit Stop, the ice cream stand where Marty had had the amazing milkshake two years earlier. The menu was written on the facade of the stand – banana splits, sundaes, parfaits, shakes, all the flavors – it was all described in detail with the associated prices. We spent a good five minutes standing in the blazing sun reading all of the options (actually, I read the entire menu to Marty because he didn't have his glasses).

Once we had made our decisions, we looked down at the window to place our orders. To our complete shock and horror, in front of the window was a handwritten sign:

AT LUNCH - BACK AT 2:30

It was only 1:00 p.m. and ninety degrees - there was no way we were going to wait an hour and a half for a milkshake. Marty was crushed.

But I wasn't ready to give up yet. I convinced Marty to take a spin thorough town to see if there were any other options. We found a diner that looked promising. We went in and asked if they made shakes. They said they no longer carried ice cream. *Shut down again.*

We rode further into town and came to an intersection. *Bingo!* On one corner we spotted a sign above a stand, with a picture of a huge, perfectly-layered vanilla ice cream cone – which Marty and I call the "International Symbol for Soft Serve." On another corner was a diner. Outside the diner was a girl, about sixteen years old, scraping ice out from a freezer that clearly had not been defrosted in a long time. We rode over toward her.

"Do you make milkshakes?" I asked.

"Yes. If you give me ten minutes, I'll make you the best milkshake of your life."

We decided to wait for the life-changing shake. The place was Donges Drive-In. From the outside it looked a bit run-down. We opened the door and were greeted by a blast of cool air. I spotted a table by the window and started walking towards it. Marty pointed at the padded stools at the counter; I nodded and joined him there.

After a few minutes, the girl came in. Another girl, about the same age, was also working there.

"What is Meyersdale known for?" Marty asked them.

"Maple," one of them answered. "Every year we have the Maple Festival, and they crown a Maple Queen. I was the Maple Queen last year. Okay, what kind of milkshakes will you have?"

"Chocolate malt for me." I kept it simple. Marty always likes to take things up a notch, though.

"What is your signature shake?" he asked.

"Maple," she answered. Of course. "We make it with maple ice cream and real local maple syrup."

"I'll have *that*," said Marty.

She dove into the ice cream buckets and dug out scoop after scoop and placed them into two aluminum tins, then added the flavorings and spun them under the spinner. She poured them out into two huge cups, added whipped cream and then set the tins with the remainder of the shakes next to the cups.

We started into them. The first sip was incredible, and we agreed they were the best shakes we'd ever had (later we decided that the heat of the day, plus the events of the hour leading up to the shake, may have thrown off our judgement). We finished off the shakes in no time, and quickly ordered two more. This time they were black raspberry and strawberry. Of all of them, we agreed that maple shake was the best.

Marty with maple milkshake, Donges Diner,
Meyersdale, PA

"What makes these shakes so amazing?" I asked the girls.

"Each one has six scoops of ice cream," she answered.

Marty and I looked at each other in disbelief. Each of us had just consumed twelve scoops of ice cream, plus the milk, flavorings and whipped cream. And we still had about twenty-five miles ahead of us, uphill, in ninety-degree heat. Perhaps a judgement error, but it was worth every calorie.

Satisfied, we got back on our bikes and ascended out of town up to the GAP trail. The trail was fully exposed to the sun, with wide open fields on both sides. The grade was about 2% uphill, just enough to ensure we felt those shakes in our stomachs. After about fifteen miles, we hit the Eastern Continental Divide - the place where water to the east flows into the Chesapeake Bay and Atlantic Ocean, and to the west flows into the Ohio River and the Gulf of Mexico.

Eastern Continental Divide

A few miles later, we reached the top of Big Savage Mountain. At 2400 feet elevation, this was the highest point of our ride. At the top of the mountain is a former railroad tunnel which now allows bikes - the Big Savage Tunnel. It was nearly a mile long and dark inside, but we made our way through with the help of lights we had clipped onto our bikes.

Big Savage Tunnel

Upon exiting the tunnel, we were met with a stunning view. A vast valley stretched out below, and we could see for over twenty miles. We stopped for a bit to take in the vista and relieve the cramping from the shakes. By now it was around 4:00 p.m. and we were getting ready to call it a day. Fortunately, we had only five miles to go, and they were downhill.

View from the Eastern side of the Big Savage Tunnel

We got back on our bikes and began coasting. Along the way, we crossed over the Mason-Dixon Line and into Maryland. Within 20 minutes, we would be in Frostburg, where we would end Day 2 and stay for the night.

Mason-Dixon Line: Crossing from Pennsylvania to Maryland

19

NO USER FEE

Marty was just ahead of me as we made our way down toward Frostburg. My eyes were drawn to the small bag mounted on the back of his bike. I recalled that inside – just as in my bag – was a single pair of shorts and two or three T-shirts for the evenings, along with an extra set of bike clothes. When I travel for work, even for an overnight trip, I typically have a rolling bag with lots of extra clothes, toiletries and other things I don't really need. It was liberating knowing we could travel 335 miles over five days using just the power of our legs, and with just a small eight-pound bag.

I thought about how Marty always dresses casually and rarely even wears long pants. For Marty, packing "just the essentials" was not as much of a challenge.

It reminded me of the time when Belle and Katie's youngest brother, Joe, was graduating from Georgetown University in Washington, DC in 2001.

~

That weekend, Katie's entire family came into town for the big event, and Belle and Marty drove down from Pittsburgh and stayed with us. We all had tickets to the graduation ceremony in the formal hall on Georgetown campus. As usual, Marty brought his bike with him.

On Saturday morning, Katie, Belle and I were downstairs having breakfast.

"Where's Marty?" I asked.

"He went for an early bike ride," Belle answered.

A few minutes later, Marty returned, sweating profusely.

"How far did you ride?" I asked.

"I did about thirty miles," Marty answered. "It's beautiful out there. Starting to get hot, though."

"Do you guys want to go ahead and shower?" Katie asked. "We need to leave in about two hours to head into Georgetown and get good seats."

I followed Belle and Marty upstairs.

"Marty, what are you wearing to the graduation?" Belle asked him.

"What do you mean?" asked Marty.

Belle was watching as I laid out my suit on the bed and looked into my closet to choose a tie.

"Did you bring a suit or sport coat?" Belle asked Marty.

"No, why?"

"*Are you serious?*" Belle was in disbelief. "We are going to a formal event and the whole family will be there! *All you have are T-shirts and shorts?*"

"Belle, it's hot out. Plus you never said there was anything formal about this weekend."

"It's a *graduation*! Graduations are formal. Everyone knows that!" Belle was frustrated.

Marty shrugged his shoulders. "I do have this polo shirt. That would work. But all I have are shorts – no pants."

"I wish I could help," I chimed in. "But I don't have anything that would fit Marty."

"Jimmy, do you think you could take Marty to a store nearby so he can buy a pair of pants?"

"Sure," I agreed. "Marty, let's go, we don't have a lot of time."

We got in my car and headed to the closest store, a K-mart about ten minutes away. We went in and found the men's section. They had jeans, shorts, and a section of Docker's khaki pants for around $25. Bingo.

"How about these?" I asked.

"Yeah, those would work."

Marty flipped through the stacks of Dockers and found a pair in his size. He tried them on and decided that they looked okay. He paid for them at the register and we headed home.

"Belle, what do you think?" Marty asked as he showed her the new pants.

"Those are fine. You don't have a jacket but at least you won't look like you walked in off the street."

We drove down to Georgetown, attended the graduation and had a great time. Back at our house, we stayed up late playing cards and having fun.

The next morning, we finished breakfast and Belle and Marty started to pack up the car to head back to Pittsburgh.

"Hey Jimbo, do you think we could make a quick trip back to K-mart before we leave?" Marty asked.

I was puzzled. "Why?"

"I want to return those Dockers."

"What don't you like about them?"

"Nothing. I just don't need them anymore."

I couldn't tell if he was serious. "Haha, that's good, Marty."

"No, really, let's head back there," Marty insisted.

"Marty, how will you explain the reason you don't need them?"

"I've had them for less than twenty-four hours. I don't think they'll need a reason."

I reluctantly agreed and we drove back to K-mart. Marty presented the pants at the register.

Predictably, the clerk asked, "Is there anything wrong with the pants, sir?"

"No," replied Marty, shaking his head while maintaining direct eye contact with the clerk.

The clerk looked at Marty, then back at the pants, and then proceeded to process the return. He handed Marty the receipt. Marty grabbed it, looked at me and said quietly and with a wry smile:

"Look, Jimbo. No user fee."

20

TEN PERCENT OFF

Back on the trail, we coasted another few miles and arrived at Frostburg. We had 135 miles behind us and 200 miles to go.

We had to climb a steep hill to get from the trail to our hotel – by way of a number of switchbacks which led higher and higher, a cruel way to end a long day of riding.

We found our hotel – The Trail Inn. It was a rustic place with exposed timber beams on the outside and two levels of rooms, all of which open to an outside balcony. At first, there seemed to be no one there. We looked in the office and walked around the place but could not find a soul. No cars in the parking lot – it appeared to be empty. Finally, a harried woman in her thirties appeared, carrying a wireless phone.

"Hi, do you work here?" I asked.

"Yes, can I help you?" she answered.

"I made a reservation for a room for tonight."

She looked through the files in the desk in the office and shook her head. Marty and I looked at each other. Then she called someone using her wireless phone. We could hear part of the conversation but couldn't fully make out what was being discussed. She hung up.

"Yes, Mr. Shea, I just spoke with the owner. Your room is on the second floor." I am not sure how she selected that particular room, or why we had to walk up to the second floor, as there was literally no one else around.

"Thanks," I said.

"And we have a restaurant which is open until 8:00 p.m... *and I've been authorized to give you both ten percent off all your food and your booze.*"

This sounded odd to us – why a ten percent discount? And who authorized it? *Booze?* We laughed a little uncertainly. "Thanks – we may take you up on that."

We walked upstairs and found our room. I showered first, which felt great. While Marty was showering, I walked downstairs and found the woman in the restaurant, which was a small kitchen with four or five tables. She showed me the menu. My eyes focused on the beer section. Sam Adams, Bud, Iron City, and a few other choices. Sam Adams was three dollars a bottle which I thought was a deal.

"I'll have a Sam Adams," I said.

She opened the ice-cold beer and handed it to me. "They're three dollars each, but with ten percent off, that's... well, just give me two dollars."

"Sure," I said. Given that she was rounding down, I figured now was the time to order more. I got one for Marty, and then ordered another round for each of us.

When Marty appeared, we sat down and enjoyed the beers while discussing where we should have dinner. We looked at the Trail Inn dinner menu. It looked good – burgers and sandwiches – and with our generous discount it was enticing. However, since we'd be eating breakfast at the

Inn the next morning, we thought we'd find something different in town.

Train Station in Frostburg, MD

Frostburg is home to Frostburg State University. In three weeks, the town would be bustling with college students, but in early August, there were not many people around. We walked up and down Main Street and asked someone for a recommendation for dinner.

"The best place in town is that Mexican place down the street."

We were still burping up Mexican food from our lunch the previous day, but since it came highly recommended, we figured we would have it again.

We paid no attention to the sign on the door, sat down and opened the menu. We were stunned. The menus looked exactly the same as El Canelo, the place in Connellsville.

There it was – the first item at the top left – the Speedy Gonzales. Same price – $5.95.

"Do you think there is a standard package you get when you want to open a Mexican restaurant, with stock menus and the same set of choices?" Marty asked me.

"That's crazy. It is too coincidental," I replied. We looked at the name of the restaurant on the menu – *El Canelo.* Were we in the twilight zone?

Our waitress came over, and I needed to know.

"Do you happen to have another restaurant in Connellsville, Pennsylvania?" I thought to myself but didn't say "... *with a guy who says 'yes my friend' all the time?*"

"Yes," she answered. "That's my brother's place."

What are the odds of that? We ordered something other than the Speedy Gonzales to mix it up a little, and then walked through town, slowly making our way back to the Trail Inn.

21

THE DUMPSTER

Frostburg is an interesting place. Just over the Maryland-Pennsylvania border, it has a distinctive western Pennsylvania vibe – mountains, coal mines, Iron City Beer, and even a hint of the Pittsburgh accent. It is only a ninety minute drive from Pittsburgh (and 2.5 hours from Washington, DC). It feels like it should be "Steeler Country."

However, for many years, Frostburg was the home of the Washington Redskins (now the Football Team) summer training camp. As you walk through town, you still see lots of Redskins signs and memorabilia, a nod to the team that drew crowds every August for years.

I grew up as a Redskins fan. I remember watching Sonny Jurgensen, Billy Kilmer, Darrell Green and Art Monk. But when I moved to Pittsburgh in 2003, I gradually became a Steeler fan. In 2007, my parents came from Arlington to visit us for Thanksgiving in Pittsburgh. That Saturday the Redskins were playing the Steelers at Heinz Field. I bought tickets and brought my dad to the game. I remember cheering for the Steelers while my dad cheered for the Redskins. The transformation was complete.

As we walked through Frostburg, I began recalling our move from Maryland to Pittsburgh in 2003. I had started my new job a few weeks before our family moved, so I stayed with Belle and Marty for the first week before moving into temporary housing.

~

Belle and Marty live in a 130-year-old house in Friendship, a neighborhood in the East End of the city of Pittsburgh. For many years, the house was Marty's summer project. As an artist, he renovated the entire house room-by-room, and over time it became his work of art.

Since the house was built in the 1800s, it has virtually no insulation, and in the wintertime Belle and Marty never run the furnace or the gas bill would be astronomical. Instead they run a pellet stove, which is a modern version of a wood-burning stove. In the depths of the Pittsburgh winters in Marty's house, you need to be within ten feet of the pellet stove or you risk hypothermia. Before visiting them in the winter, Katie and I would always call ahead for the forecast – *inside* their house.

"Marty, what's it looking like over there?" I would ask.

"Well, it's about forty-five degrees, with a southeasterly breeze about ten miles an hour coming out of the kitchen," Marty would say jokingly. But I knew this meant bundling up and wearing a sweater or a hoodie in the house.

When I started my new job in Pittsburgh, it was August and it was hot. Of course, Belle and Marty's house also has no air conditioning. To create some air flow they leave their windows open, which means that all night long while you lay in bed sweating you hear a symphony of sirens, honking horns and people yelling at each other. Coming from a quiet suburban cul-de-sac in Maryland, I was not used to this.

"Marty, how do you sleep with all this noise?" I asked.

"You need to chill out, Jimbo. Think of it like camping in the 'hood. If you are in chill mode, you won't have any trouble sleeping."

The next morning, I came downstairs in my suit and found Marty on the front porch, shirtless, drinking coffee and reading the newspaper. I hadn't slept well and needed coffee. Marty poured me a cup and I began putting on my tie.

As we sat on the porch drinking our coffees, I noticed a station wagon parked on the side of the house.

"You see that car, Jimbo?" Marty asked.

"Yeah, what about it?"

"See what's inside it?" Marty pointed as he took a sip of his coffee.

I squinted and looked closer. The entire back half of the station wagon was filled with garbage – drywall, wood, rags, even some old light fixtures.

"What's up with that?" I asked.

Marty set down his cup. "Jimbo, that car has been sitting there for months. Someone just abandoned it there. I've called the city multiple times to get them to tow it, but they've done nothing."

I listened as Marty continued: "I finally went out there a few days ago and found that the back of the wagon was left open. And you know that room I'm renovating upstairs? Well, I have all this stuff to get rid of and I don't have a dumpster. So I opened the back lift gate and started filling it up. That thing is packed to the gills with all the debris from that room."

I was speechless. "So you are just using that station wagon as your personal dumpster?"

"You got it, Jimbo."

The next day, after another night of broken sleep (for me), we were again sitting on the front porch drinking coffee before I headed to work. Just then, from two blocks away, we saw a middle-aged man walking slowly down the middle of the street toward Belle and Marty's house. He walked with a slight limp and was clearly in no hurry. We watched as, to our surprise, he approached the station wagon. He opened the driver's door, plopped in the seat, started the engine, and drove away.

He never looked in the back of the car nor did he seem troubled by it in the least.

We tried to put together what must have happened. Marty finally concluded that he must have been in jail for the last three months and had come to reclaim his car.

"Perfect. Now all that junk is gone, *and* the car is gone," Marty chuckled. "And I never had to get a dumpster."

22

CHEESING VS CHILLIN'

Back in Frostburg, I slept well in our room at the Trail Inn as I was tired after two days of riding. I woke up the next morning before Marty and headed downstairs to get some coffee. The sun was just coming up over the mountain and its morning rays were illuminating the front of the Inn.

I found a chair and sat down facing the sunrise. I was all alone, and I again began thinking of our move to Pittsburgh in 2003 and that week-long stay at Belle and Marty's house.

∾

On Friday, the last day of my first week on my new job, Marty and I were again on the front porch drinking coffee. It had been a tough transition and I was ready for the weekend. For Marty, it was just another day of his endless summer. I was in my work attire – dress shirt, slacks and wing tips. Marty was in his summer uniform – T-shirt, shorts and sandals. Before heading off, I looked at him on the sofa. He was clearly very relaxed.

"So, what exactly do you do all day, Marty?" I asked. "Just sit around cheesing on the sofa?"

"Yo, Jimbo, does this look like cheesing? It is far from it. I am *chillin'*."

"Cheesing... Chilling... it's all the same, right? You're just sitting around!"

"Well, there is a *big* difference, Jimbo," argued Marty. He went on to explain: "I have spent the last two months since school let out in June working my way into this deep state of super-chill. I am to the point now where nothing bothers me. You know those sounds that keep you up at night? I don't even hear them."

"Yeah, but you are just cheesing away all day, doing nothing."

"Far from it, Jimbo," said Marty. "This is *purposeful* relaxation. Every moment has a purpose to it. I make coffee, I go to the bakery, I walk the dog, I read the paper. Sometimes I look at the people walking by on the sidewalk... it all has a purpose. It's *chillin'*."

"Let me show you something," said Marty as he got up from the sofa. I followed him into the basement where his sons were playing a video game. They were glued to the TV with their hand-held controllers and didn't even notice us entering the room.

"You see this?" said Marty, pointing at the boys. "Now *that's cheesing.*"

"Okay..."

"This mindless video game – it has no purpose. Look at their eyes – glazed over. They don't even know we're standing here. This is a complete waste of time – it is *cheesing.*"

"And when you sit on the sofa watching people go by, that has a purpose?"

"Of course – I am in the moment, participating in life. It has a purpose, and I am *chillin'*."

Well, Marty actually did a lot more during those summers than just chill. He spent hours each day working on his house, renovating bedrooms and bathrooms, painting, and laying floor tile. It was a labor of love, and as an artist, Marty turned the house into his own form of sculpture. But while he worked, he maintained his deep state of "super-chill."

A decade later, after Marty had essentially renovated the entire house, there was still one ceramic tile missing in their kitchen floor. It remained that way for years. During one visit to Belle and Marty's house, Katie asked about it.

"Marty, the house is gorgeous, but when are you going to put in this last tile?"

"He won't do it," replied Belle.

"Why?" I asked.

"Fear of death," said Belle.

Marty laughed and nodded. After ten years of working on the house, it had become a part of him, and that last tile represented the last step of a project he couldn't bear to complete.

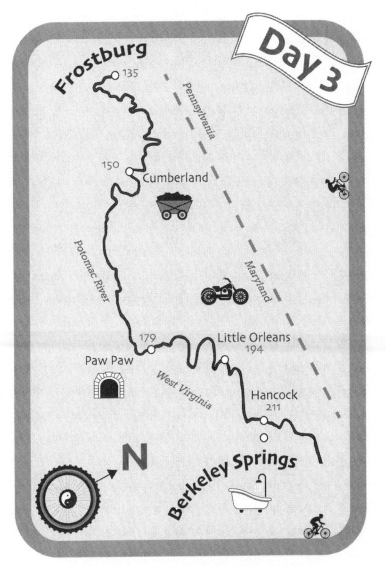

Frostburg, Md to Berkeley Springs, WVa

23

COASTING

I n Frostburg, Marty woke up about an hour after me and found me downstairs at the café in the Trail Inn.

"Any luck?" I asked as he joined me at the table.

"Nada," said Marty, shaking his head dejectedly. We were now well outside his thirty mile radius, and I suspected this could become an issue as we continued to consume vast quantities of food.

Speaking of food, the same woman who had checked us in the night before offered us breakfast. This time she was wearing an apron with her name sewn on it – Rachel. She handed each of us a sheet of paper with the meal choices, along with a small pencil.

As usual, Marty handed me his sheet, and I read off the choices to him – western omelet, pancakes, bacon, corned beef hash, toast... I read Marty's mind and started making check marks with my pencil next to every item on both sheets.

Rachel approached our table and I handed her our sheets.

"You *both* want *everything*?"

"Yes, is that a problem?" I replied.

"Not as long as you eat it all," she said.

She took our sheets back to the kitchen. Ten minutes later, the food started coming... and coming. We had clearly ordered too much but ate every bit of it under Rachel's watchful eye.

We were completely stuffed. On one hand, since this was to be a very long day (seventy-six miles), we were glad we had packed away the calories to fuel our trip. On the other hand, we could barely move and were afraid we'd give back our breakfasts on the trail within the first few miles.

Marty leaving the Trail Inn, Frostburg, MD

We mounted our bikes, rode back down the switchback and rejoined the trail. Fortunately, the day started with a fifteen-mile descent down Big Savage Mountain with a grade of 4%. We coasted and took in the scenery. As we glided downhill, we passed a few bikers who had started their trek in DC and were struggling as they worked their way uphill.

About halfway down the mountain, the trail makes a

wide, sweeping bend as it hugs the mountain, known as Helmstetter's Curve. When the railroad was running in the early 1900s, passengers in the front of the train could see the back of the train and vice versa. Now no longer in service, a replica of the train runs from Cumberland to Frostburg, giving tourists the feeling of what passengers experienced a century ago.

Helmstetter's Curve near Cumberland, MD

Downhill stretch from Frostburg to Cumberland, MD

As we coasted, Marty and I chatted.

"Hey Jimbo, I meant to tell you, I'm going on a fishing trip with Sam up in Canada after we get back."

Sam is Marty's oldest son and is an avid fisherman. He goes on a week-long fishing trip in Canada every year with his friend Pat and Pat's father, Matt, who organizes and leads the trip. They fish for northern pike, walleye and muskie by boat in a remote area of northern Ontario.

"Sounds great, Marty. I haven't fished in a long time," I said, my eyes fixed on the rural Western Maryland landscape, a beautiful scene dotted with barns, wildflowers and corn fields.

"Yeah, Matt called me and told me to buy a rain suit for the trip. He told me the type I should buy and sent me a link – it's pretty heavy duty since they often get bad weather up there."

"Did you get it?" I asked.

"Well, I put it off, and then I saw him a week later." *Typical Marty,* I thought. *After all, he had this biking vacation to think about before the fishing vacation.* "He asked me if I'd bought the suit yet and I told him I hadn't."

"And?" I asked.

"Then I saw him again a few days after that. He asked me again if I'd bought it, and I told him I hadn't."

This did not surprise me. "So?" We were about half way down the mountain to Cumberland, pedaling easily as the trail took us through another former railroad tunnel – the Borden Tunnel.

"Well, the day before we left for this bike trip, Matt shows up at my front door and presents me with a brand new rain suit he bought for me! He asked me to try it on – it fit perfectly. I thanked him – it was really nice of him to do that."

I thought for a few seconds as Marty concluded the story of the rain suit. I looked over at him.

"Marty, yes that was certainly nice of Matt and it says a lot about him as a person. But even more importantly, do you know what else it says – about *you*?"

"That I'm a procrastinator?" Marty chimed in and laughed a little.

"Think about it. *It means you are not an asshole.*"

Marty laughed a little to humor me, but I could tell he didn't fully understand the importance of this revelation. "Yeah, I guess so," he said.

"No, Marty, really." I was trying to make a point. "Remember when we were in DC and that guy wrote that message on your back window?"

"Yeah, I know you told me what you thought it really meant, but to tell you the truth, I never really got over it," said Marty.

"Okay, think about it," I said. "Why would anyone go out and buy a rain suit for someone and then bring it over to their house for them to try on – if that person is an asshole?"

I continued: "Clearly Matt likes you and this is evidence of that. But there are a lot of assholes in this world, and this shows that you are not one of them. It should make you feel good."

Now it was Marty's turn to process this new insight. He nodded and his smile grew bigger.

"Whew!" Marty exclaimed as he wiped the back of his hand across his forehead. "I see what you mean, Jimbo! Lots of people go through life worried about whether or not they're an asshole. I was never sure myself given that message on my window. What a relief!"

"Exactly," I said.

Marty glowed and nodded approvingly. I could see how good this thought made him feel.

"Well, Jimbo, the air smells a little sweeter right now knowing what that rain suit really means."

Of course, what it really meant was that Matt didn't want the fishing trip to be delayed by a side trip to the outfitter store on the drive up to Canada. But I went ahead and let Marty enjoy the moment.

About thirty minutes later, we coasted into Cumberland, Maryland. Here the GAP trail ends and the C&O Canal trail begins. We had 150 miles behind us, and 185 miles to go.

24

CUMBERLAND

Cumberland sits on the North Fork of the Potomac River and is built on the site of the mid-eighteenth century Fort Cumberland, the starting point for General Braddock's march on Fort Duquesne in 1755. Cumberland also served as an outpost for George Washington during the French and Indian War, and his first military headquarters was built there once he became a Colonel.

From Cumberland, the Potomac River flows to Washington, DC and eventually to the Chesapeake Bay, growing continually wider along the way. Between Cumberland and Harpers Ferry, West Virginia, the Potomac forms the border between Maryland and West Virginia. From Harpers Ferry to the Chesapeake, the Potomac separates Maryland and Virginia. The river was the primary dividing line between the Union and the Confederacy for the Eastern Theater of the Civil War.

As a young man, George Washington was focused on navigating the Potomac because it was viewed as the best pathway to the Ohio Country, into which his employer wanted to expand. After the Revolutionary War, Washington returned to private enterprise and, together with Thomas Jefferson, formed the Patowmack Company with a similar objective – to develop a pathway to Pittsburgh. Washington employed surveyors and concluded that the distance between DC and Pittsburgh was approximately 360 miles – not far off from the 335 miles Marty and I were traversing.

While the Potomac contained many stretches of flat, calm water, there were also several areas such as Harpers Ferry, Great Falls and Little Falls where rough water rendered it impractical to navigate. Washington and the Patowmack Company developed a plan to dig short "skirting canals" which would enable a boat to avoid these rapids. Several of these canals were well underway when Washington became President of the United States, at which point the work slowed down. The last skirting canal was completed around Great Falls in 1802, three years after Washington's death.

Two decades later, the Chesapeake and Ohio (C&O) company was formed with a goal of digging a canal from DC all the way to Pittsburgh. Work started in 1828, about the same time the Baltimore & Ohio (B&O) railroad began laying tracks with a similar objective. The canal was completed as far as Cumberland in 1850, and by that point, the railroad was also fully operational. The railroad – deemed to be a more efficient means of transportation – continued on to Pittsburgh and additional work on the canal stopped.

The canal prospered for about thirty years, and in 1880, the B&O acquired the canal, primarily to keep the right-of-way from falling into the hands of a competing railroad. The B&O operated it at a loss for another forty years and officially closed it in 1924. In 1938 it was sold to the U.S. Government for $2 million and became a National Historic Park in 1971.

While the canal was in operation, as many as 500 boats worked the waterway, shuttling crops and people up and down the Potomac. During the Civil War, Union forces used it to move troops and war supplies.

But the canal's major source of revenue was carrying coal. The hills around Cumberland were abundant in two types of coal – bituminous and anthracite. Bituminous coal burns fast and hot and could be made into coke which was used to fire steel mills. Anthracite coal burns slower and at lower temperatures, and its higher carbon content also means it burns cleaner. Anthracite coal was primarily used for home heating and cooking.

Downtown Cumberland, MD

The steel industry in Pittsburgh in the late 1800s had a constant need for Cumberland's bituminous coal. Because the canal stopped in Cumberland, the railroad that once occupied the GAP trail carried Cumberland coal to

Connellsville, where coke was made, and then on to Pittsburgh to the steel mills.

Around this same time, the population of Washington, DC was growing quickly, and there was an insatiable appetite for anthracite coal for home use. Cumberland coal was ideal, and the canal was an efficient way to transport it. Barges full of coal made their way from Cumberland to Washington, pulled by mules on a towpath which ran alongside the canal.

When building the canal, the engineers faced a significant challenge: Cumberland was at 600 feet elevation and DC was at sea level. How to account for the difference so that the water in the canal would stay level?

Designers created a lock system which would allow a barge to enter, then close behind it while the water would be released into the canal below it. Once the barge had been lowered to the next level (approximately eight feet), the downstream canal door would open, and the barge would continue until the next lock. The locks also worked in the reverse direction for a barge headed upstream. In total, seventy-four locks were installed, each one accommodating an eight foot change in elevation, for a total of 600 feet.

∽

This lock system provided an unexpected benefit for Marty and me in 2010. Riding from Cumberland to DC would be 185 miles on the same towpath walked by the mules in the 1880s. Since the towpath ran alongside the canal, this meant that we would enjoy these eight-foot descents, one every two or three miles (similar to being rewarded with a short page of text at the end of each chapter, like in this book).

This was a pleasant treat which those riding the other

direction did not have the opportunity to enjoy.

We stopped briefly at the visitor's center in Cumberland to learn about the canal, then rode through the city. Cumberland was once the second largest city in Maryland, known as the Queen City. Like many of the towns we had passed through over the last two days, it experienced a decline during the 1900's. However, Cumberland's location at the nexus of the GAP and C&O trails has created a renaissance in the city, and there are now shops and restaurants in Canal Place and along its pretty cobblestone Centre street.

We headed for the C&O. Once on the trail, we immediately missed the pristine condition of the GAP trail. The towpath, of course, was not built to be a bike trail and hasn't seen much improvement since the days when mules walked it. It was full of ruts and mud puddles, and occasional rocks and grass. Biking it required more attention and focus.

We felt energized after coming off the fifteen mile descent from Frostburg and decided to kick into high gear. Marty set the pace and I was working hard to keep up. As we rode along in between the canal and the Potomac, the miles were clicking by.

Suddenly, my front tire hit a rut in the path which I hadn't seen. My tire was caught for a split second, and my body launched over the handlebars. Thankfully, I was thrown to the left instead of straight ahead. I landed in some tall grass to the side of the path.

I lay there for a few seconds, checking to make sure I hadn't broken anything.

"What happened?" asked Marty as he rode back to help me.

"Hit a rut and took a spill. I'm okay."

I got up, and other than a few minor cuts, I was fine. We decided to take it a little slower from that point.

Marty at Lock 74 on the C&O Canal

After another mile – now about five miles outside of Cumberland – we saw an unusual sight. We had gotten used to going miles and miles without seeing anyone. Here, on the towpath, were two SWAT SUVs, one parked in front of the other. We slowed down and rode our bikes past them. Just as we were passing them, we saw four men in bullet proof vests taking semi-automatic rifles out of the SUVs.

We rode up the path another twenty or thirty yards, then stopped and looked back. The canal bed was dry there, and we watched as the SWAT officers worked their way across the canal bed and up the other side. They slowly headed toward a small shack in the woods about fifty yards past the canal. They stopped outside the shack, waited, and then entered. We waited for a little while, but they did not re-emerge. Then we got back on our bikes and started imagining what it might have happened.

25

BILL'S PLACE

We rode the canal towpath, taking in the scenery along the Potomac as it snaked its way around hills and made its way downstream toward Washington. At some points the now-defunct canal would be completely dry; at others it would contain some standing water with algae. In these spots, fallen trees would often protrude from the stagnant water in the canal. On many of these exposed branches, terrapin turtles would rest and bask in the sun. We saw hundreds of them. And every two or three miles we would have a welcome eight-foot drop as we passed over a lock.

Around noon, near Paw Paw, West Virginia, we emerged from underneath the cool, treed canopy and the topography changed. Along the right side of the trail was a huge rock wall with beautiful orange and brown colors. The canal to our left contained about a foot of water at this point. In front of us was a mountain. The builders of the canal had faced a choice here: run the canal around the mountain or blow a hole and go straight through. They chose the direct path and dug a tunnel through the mountain.

The Paw Paw tunnel has a narrow bike path on the right side of the canal and is completely dark inside. We started into the tunnel on our bikes, but quickly dismounted once the darkness set in. We had small lights which helped guide us, and every so often we would shine them on the water in the canal to the left. Other than the sound of our shoes, the tunnel was silent and was about ten degrees cooler than the outside air. At one point we passed two bikers heading the other direction. It was a tight squeeze to let them pass.

Paw Paw Tunnel, near Paw Paw, WV

We emerged on the other side, back in the sun, got back on our bikes and rode away.

As usual, we got hungry and thirsty. On the map, I noticed a small town called Little Orleans, Maryland and thought that would be a good place to stop. We arrived there and got off the trail. In order to enter the town, we needed to go through a small tunnel. The tunnel also contained three or four men riding Harleys, revving their engines and reveling in the roaring echoes created by the tunnel. Our bikes were unable to contribute to the din.

On the other side of the tunnel, we were surprised by a full battalion of Harleys. The town was literally full of Harleys.

"Town" is a bit of a stretch. Little Orleans consisted of "Bill's Place" – a small bar/restaurant which also sold groceries and bait & tackle. Across the road was a smoker stand under a tent serving pit beef sandwiches (also run by Bill), and a tattoo stand (run by – you guessed it – Bill).

We opted for Bill's Place. There were about twenty Harleys parked outside the bar. We found an open spot and parked our bikes in between them. Then we walked toward the bar in our tight bike clothing, attracting attention as the cleats on the bottom of our bike shoes clicked and clacked up the steps.

Little Orleans, MD (our bikes are on the right)

We opened the door and let our eyes adjust to the darkness. Inside we saw a bar where about ten Harley riders were sitting, as well as a few tables where no one was sitting. I suggested a table in the corner, so we could keep our distance from the Harley guys, but Marty wanted to sit at the bar to get the "local flavor." So we sat at the bar.

Behind the bar were hung several rifles and deer heads, a picture of Osama Bin Laden with a target drawn on his forehead, and a sign that said:

**THIS IS NOT BURGER KING. YOU GET
THE SON-OF-A-BITCH OUR WAY
OR YOU DON'T GET IT AT ALL.**

Needless to say, in my neon shirt and spandex shorts, I felt a little out of place.

"What'll ya have?" asked the bartender.

"How about two bananas and two Diet Cokes?" said Marty.

The bartender raised his eyebrows, then turned around to look for some bananas. The Harley riders on our left chuckled a little.

"What are you guys doing?" one of them asked, taking a swig of his beer.

"Riding to DC – on bicycles. How about you?" Marty was already engaging them.

"We're here for the rally," one of them replied.

"What rally?" I asked.

"Bill here owns 400 acres up over that hill, and every August we all come here and hang out for the week." He said that it's the biggest Harley rally east of the Mississippi – they call it "East Coast Sturgis." Over 3,000 people attend –

everyone sleeps in tents, they have demolition derbies and pretty much do whatever they want.

We finished up our bananas and Diet Cokes. I needed to use the restroom, so Marty headed outside. By the time I got out there, Marty was talking to a sunburned woman in her forties with long black hair. She was wearing a tank top and had bandages on both shoulders. He was showing her our bikes.

"Don't you ever wish you had a motor on that thing?" she asked, slurring her words. She was either drunk or stoned or maybe both.

We laughed. "It's a lot of effort, for sure," I said. "*What happened to your arms?*"

"Just got two new tattoos. Wanna see them?"

"No... that's okay... please don't..."

But it was too late. She was already peeling one of the bandages off, revealing a freshly painted rose along with something else we couldn't make out due to all the blood.

"What's up with this Harley rally?" Marty asked.

"Well, we just get naked and smoke pot for a week. Wanna come?"

I am 100% sure Marty would have gone had I not been there.

"Thanks for the invite," I said. "We gotta get to Berkeley Springs before dark so we're going to have to pass."

Marty looked at me, then back at her and at the line of Harleys. He clearly wanted to stay.

"Come on Marty." I was the voice of reason. "There are beers and a bed waiting for us in Berkeley Springs."

Reluctantly, Marty agreed. We said goodbye to her, to Bill's Place and to Little Orleans and got back on the trail.

26

THE MANGO CHUTNEY

Upon departing Little Orleans, we had completed fifty-nine miles on our third day, with seventeen miles to go. It was mid-afternoon, and the August heat and humidity were relentless.

As we rode along, I began thinking of fall and imagined these woods turning gold, red and brown in two short months. I loved the fall in Pennsylvania and Maryland – the cool, crisp mornings and bright, sunny days with low humidity.

~

Marty and I like traditions. Over the last few years we developed a fall tradition – we'd meet for a burger on the patio of the Bettis Grille in Pittsburgh on the last seventy degree day of the year. This typically fell in late October or early November.

The Bettis Grille is a sports bar owned by Jerome Bettis, the Steeler's legendary Hall of Fame running back. The restaurant has an outdoor patio which sits on the North Shore of the Ohio

River, directly across from The Point. It is also situated between Heinz Field and PNC Park, and boasts a great view down the Ohio River where the sun sets in the valley before you.

Marty and I sit on the patio, get a couple of burgers and beers, and reminisce about the summer as we watch the sun set. Within a few days the weather turns colder and the long Pittsburgh winter starts.

At the end of October 2009, Marty and I were watching the weather and saw the forecast we were looking for – the first week of November was expected to be seventy degrees and sunny. It was time for our annual Bettis Grille trip.

I met Marty at the restaurant. There was no one else sitting outside, and we were not entirely sure they were still serving customers on the patio given that it was late in the season. But we found a table and sat down anyway. Within a few minutes, a waiter came outside.

"Can we eat out here?" I asked.

"Sure," said the waiter. Can I bring you some drinks?" He handed us our menus.

We ordered two IPAs and started looking at the menus. The waiter went inside and soon came back out with our beers.

"I see you've had a chance to look at the menus," said the waiter. "Before you get too far, let me tell you about the special. Our special tonight is a bison burger. It comes with a fantastic mango chutney on top and a side of fries. It's really good."

Marty and I looked at each other. "You ever had bison, Jimbo?" he asked me.

"No, but it sounds interesting. Sure, why not." I was feeling adventurous.

"Two bison burgers?" asked the waiter.

"Yeah, make it two, we'll give it a try," said Marty.

The waiter took our menus and again disappeared inside.

Marty and I sipped our beers as the sun started its descent, cascading down Mount Washington toward the Ohio River. We talked about the summer, the trip to the beach, and about plans for the annual family gathering at Thanksgiving in a few weeks.

We were getting hungry. Just then, another server (not our waiter) came out and delivered our burgers. They were a thing of beauty – caramelized buns, with lettuce and tomato and a heaping portion of fries on the side.

"Dig in!" said Marty.

The first couple of bites were fantastic. They tasted like beef to us – maybe with a slightly different texture. We were thoroughly enjoying our dinners when our waiter emerged from inside and walked over to our table.

"Gentlemen, how is everything?" He asked, smiling.

"Great!" we mumbled, our mouths full.

"Excellent," said the waiter. He was watching us closely as we ate. Then his expression changed and his brow furrowed.

"Uh... wait a minute," he interrupted. "Those burgers, did they come with the mango chutney?"

We set down our burgers and lifted the buns off the top. No mango chutney.

"I guess not," I said. "But it's fine – they're great."

"No they are *not* great," declared the waiter. "The mango chutney totally makes those burgers. I was the one who told you those burgers would have mango chutney on them, and they don't. I am so sorry."

"Don't worry about it – we're fine," said Marty.

"Excuse me," said the waiter, and he turned and walked briskly back inside.

Marty and I shrugged. We continued eating and were having a great time. We were halfway through our burgers when a tall man in a suit and tie came out and appeared at our table, his hands clasped behind his back.

"Gentlemen, I am the manager," he said in a serious tone. "I have been informed about the mango chutney. Let me apologize on behalf of the Bettis Grille."

Marty and looked at each other silently as we continued chewing.

The manager continued: "Gentlemen, we will be buying your dinners tonight. In addition, the next time you come in, dinner is on us. Please accept my apology."

We were speechless. "Um... okay... thanks. But really, it's fine," I said.

The manager presented us with two vouchers good for two free dinners, and we received no bill for dinner that night.

We finished up and I drove home. A great end to the summer of 2009.

Thanksgiving was three weeks later. It was a wonderful day with about eighty relatives at our house for dinner. The day after Thanksgiving would have been our annual guys' trip to the Stoney's brewery. But that ended a few years before, and we needed a new tradition. So we started what became an annual pub crawl night on Pittsburgh's Southside, complete with a party bus and driver.

After several stops, our group of about ten guys went to a wine bar in the Southside Works. Marty and I walked into the bar together. It was loud and packed with people. As we entered, a bouncer was standing just inside the doorway. I made eye contact with him briefly as we passed by – he looked familiar to me. Our group found a big table in the bar, and I headed to the men's room. While in the restroom, I started thinking about the bouncer. I knew him from somewhere – *but where?* Just then... *bingo!* It hit me! He was our waiter from the Bettis Grille!

I rushed back to our table. I couldn't wait to tell Marty.

"See that bouncer over by the door?" I nodded my head in his direction.

"Yeah, what about him?" asked Marty.

"We both know him from somewhere," I said.

"We do? Where?"

"Keep looking at him and try to figure it out," I said.

Marty was intrigued. He looked at the guy while stroking his chin. But he could not come up with an answer.

"I'll buy the rest of your drinks tonight if you can figure out how we know him," I said.

Now it was a personal challenge. Marty wracked his brain, alternating between staring at the man and holding his head in his hands. He could not figure it out. It consumed him for the next thirty minutes while the rest of the group engaged in lively conversation about Thanksgiving.

As we were preparing to leave the bar, I said, "Well, it looks like you're not going to get it, so I'll have to tell you."

I reached into my back pocket and pulled out my wallet. I opened the billfold and began pulling out a card – the free dinner voucher from the Bettis Grille. As I was pulling it out, Marty yelled out, "The Bettis Grille! Our waiter from the Bettis Grille!"

"Yes!" I said, "But you were too late. The card gave it away."

"No it didn't!" Marty insisted. "I got it just before I saw the card!"

"I don't think so," I disagreed.

"I did!" Marty insisted.

To this day, ten years later, we still debate who was right that night. But since I am writing the book and Marty is not, I can confidently say that he saw the card and the card gave it away.

One thing we both agree on is that the mango chutney clearly cost the bouncer his job as a waiter at the Bettis Grille.

27

WELCOME, JIM AND MARTY

Our third day on the trail continued to get hotter as the afternoon wore on. About ten miles past Little Orleans, a paved trail appeared on the other side of the canal. It was covered with a canopy of trees and lined with a stunning rock wall on the left. We crossed over and got on the asphalt. It turns out that this twenty-mile section is the Western Maryland Rail Trail which starts ten miles west of Hancock, Maryland, and runs another ten miles east. Riding on the smooth pavement in the shade was a welcome relief after hours on the rough C&O trail. We cranked up the pace, and forty-five minutes later, we arrived in Hancock. We had 211 miles behind us and 124 miles to go.

Hancock is a small town in Washington County, Maryland, the narrowest part of the state. The north-south distance from the Pennsylvania state line to the West Virginia state line is only 1.8 miles at that point. The C&O Canal passes directly through Hancock, with the Potomac River on the other side, dividing Maryland and West Virginia. Interstate Route 70, the major east-west thoroughfare running from Baltimore to Utah, also passes through the town. There are a few restaurants, hotels, gas stations and shops.

Tonight we would stay at the Manor Inn, a B&B in Berkeley Springs, West Virginia, about five miles south of Hancock. Ellen, the Inn's owner, had offered to pick us up at the bike shop just off the trail. We made our way to the shop and called Ellen.

While we waited we looked around the shop. The owner said we could leave our bikes in the back, and he told us they had accommodations for trail bikers there as well. We walked our bikes around back and saw what looked like chicken coops lined up along the back wall, with a dirt courtyard in front. We focused our eyes and suddenly realized that there were humans inside them! These were the biker accommodations, each with a cot, a small table and chair, with a screen door and screen siding. There was a hose in the courtyard which they would use to get water, and a public bathroom. We talked to a couple of bikers who said they were great and were nice respite from tent camping.

We locked our bikes outside and walked back into the shop. On the wall were several WANTED posters. We took a closer look and read the text. A man had kidnapped a six-year old girl in Cumberland six days before, on August 5th. He beat the girl, then disappeared and there was a manhunt underway.

"What's up with this?" we asked the bike shop owner.

"Yeah, that guy is crazy. All the cops are looking for him from here to Cumberland. There were a few people who called with reports of having seen him on the bike trail."

We realized that our experience with the SWAT team was exactly that.

We followed the story for the next two weeks. His name

was Stephen Westfall. The girl said he had taken her from her neighborhood, had driven her to a remote, dry creek bed, hit her several times with a rock and left her for dead. She found her way to a house in Cumberland, naked, bruised and seriously beaten. She was able to describe Westfall's tattoos and the van she was taken in. The next day, police found a clip of Westfall's van on a neighborhood surveillance video. Police then spotted the van in front of a home in Cumberland and deduced that it was owned by Westfall and his girlfriend. From that moment, Westfall became the prime suspect.

By the time the police came, he was gone, but he left a note to his girlfriend. Part of it said, "No matter what happens, I love you dearly... I don't want to cause you problems."

Westfall walked and hitchhiked his way from Cumberland to Pittsburgh – the same route we had just traveled – approximately 150 miles. He then holed up with some people he knew in Pittsburgh for a few days and got some new clothes.

The following Saturday, the case was profiled on a national airing of America's Most Wanted. Westfall's girlfriend realized what he had done and was cooperating with police.

Realizing he was being pursued, he left Pittsburgh and traveled to Grantsville, Maryland (over 100 miles). On August 17th, he entered a church in Grantsville and placed a call to his girlfriend. She called the police who apprehended him.

Westfall pleaded guilty to attempted second degree murder and kidnapping. He is currently serving a fifty-five year sentence.

Back at the Hancock bike shop, Ellen soon arrived to

pick us up in a mini Cooper. Since Marty is about fifty percent bigger than me, I squeezed into the back seat, and Ellen pointed the tiny car across the Potomac River, crossing from Maryland into West Virginia and into the town of Berkeley Springs.

Berkeley Springs is a charming town full of shops, restaurants, art galleries and small hotels and B&Bs. It was originally called Bath, and in 1802 its name was changed to Berkeley Springs. The area contains mineral water springs that were frequented by Native Americans indigenous to the area, possibly for thousands of years. In 1748, George Washington, then just sixteen years old, was part of the team that surveyed this region for the British, Lord Fairfax. Washington returned several times with his half-brother, Lawrence, who was ill, in hopes that the warm springs might improve Lawrence's health.

Water flows from natural mineral springs at a constant temperature of 74.3 degrees, emerging from the Oriskany (Ridgeley) sandstone of Warm Springs Ridge. This water feeds many of the local establishments in town today, including our B&B for the night, the Manor Inn.

Ellen drove us to the Inn, a huge and beautiful Victorian house on a quiet street surrounded by shade trees. The house was painted with bright colors in pink and blue. As she parked the car, we walked up the front steps. *Click-clack, click-clack*. At the top of the steps was a gorgeous wrap-around front porch, with tables and chairs. Perfect for our breakfast tomorrow. We turned toward the front door, and on a chalkboard was written:

Welcome Jim and Marty

We knew it was a good sign.

Arriving at the Manor Inn, Berkeley Springs, WV

Upon entering the B&B we immediately smelled something baking. Ellen appeared from the kitchen with freshly-baked chocolate chip cookies. Did I mention that riding makes you hungry? We quickly devoured several of them. Then she showed us to our room, a big room with a high ceiling. We looked at the beds – one big four poster queen sized bed, and one small kid's bed on the side. Marty pointed to the kid's bed.

"Looks like that's you, Jimbo," he said.

"Why me? That bed is for little kids."

"Yeah," said Marty laughing, "It's a wee little bed."

I realized that there was no way Marty was going to fit in that "wee" bed, *and* there was no way I was sharing a bed with Marty. The choice was made.

The "wee" bed at the Manor Inn

The bathroom at the Manor Inn contained a large tub, and Ellen encouraged us to enjoy a bath in the famous Berkeley Springs mineral water. Marty and I each took a long soak, then got dressed and headed outside. There was a small park in the center of town which contained some of the original baths. The baths were outdoor concrete basins, spaced a few feet apart, fed at one end by the spring water. We imagined George Washington stretching out, enjoying a relaxing mineral bath after a long day on the battlefield.

We had dinner at a restaurant in town and walked back to the Inn. We had picked up a couple of beers and enjoyed them on the big porch.

We turned in – Marty sprawled out on the queen bed, and I folded myself into the wee bed.

The next morning, Marty was up before me. I woke up just as he was returning from the bathroom down the hall. He had a big smile on his face, pumping his fist.

"Bingo, Jimbo! Gonna be a great day!" Three days into the trip, and well outside his thirty mile radius, nature had finally taken over.

We headed downstairs. Ellen seated us for breakfast on the porch, along with a few of the other guests. She made us an incredible meal of freshly baked pastries, omelets, and an amazing fruit sculpture made of local berries.

"How did you guys sleep?" asked Ellen.

"I slept pretty well," I said. "Everything was really great, Ellen, but, uh... that second bed is a little small. Do you by any chance have a room with two twin beds for next time?"

"Um... errr..." Ellen stammered. "Of course I do! I just thought..."

In that moment Ellen realized that Marty and I were just friends. We all had a good laugh together.

We went upstairs, put on our bike clothes and packed our bags. All of the other guests had headed out for the day, and we were the last ones left in the guest house.

"We have some leftovers from breakfast – would you guys like to take them along with you for a snack on the trail?" asked Ellen.

"Sure," said Marty.

Ellen packed up all the extra food for us, and we stuffed it into our bags. Then she drove us back to the bike shop in Hancock. We said goodbye and headed back on the trail.

Breakfast at the Manor Inn

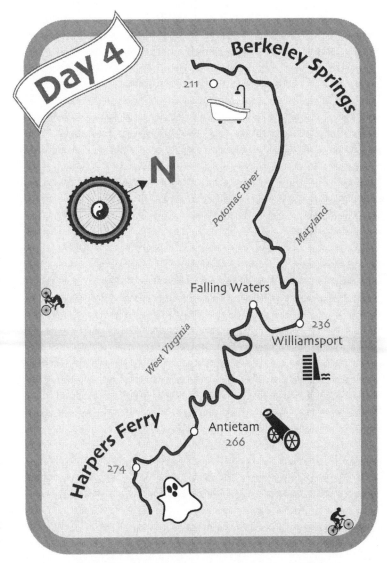

Day 4

Berkeley Springs

211

Potomac River

Maryland

N

Falling Waters

West Virginia

236
Williamsport

Harpers Ferry

Antietam
266

274

Berkeley Springs, WVa to Harpers Ferry, WVa

28

KEEPING MARTY ALIVE

Our destination today was Harpers Ferry, sixty-three miles from Hancock. We started the day with ten miles of blacktop – a continuation of the Western Maryland Rail Trail. Marty picked up the pace and I watched him accelerate like a rocket. I marveled at how fit he was for a man his age.

❧

Marty is three years older than Belle and is five years older than Katie and me. Sometimes we talk about what it will be like when we're old(er). One day this led to a discussion about who will be the first to go.

"Well, of course Marty will be the first to go," said Belle.

"Why?" asked Katie

"Because he's the oldest," reasoned Belle.

"Yeah, so since I'll be the first to go, the only thing you kids need to worry about is keeping me alive," said Marty. "As long as I'm alive, you all are in the clear."

This made perfect sense and gave all of us a sense of

peace. For Marty, this meant that the three of us would focus immense energy on making sure Marty was safe and had access to good healthcare. For the rest of us, we knew that as long as Marty was alive, we could go on living our happy lives.

Christmas is one of Marty's favorite holidays, and as we get older it is a good time to appreciate the fact that we made it through another year. For most people, Christmas involves exchanging gifts. Because Marty does not finish his working day until 2:30 p.m., often he does not have time to shop for physical gifts. Instead, he gives IOUs for the presents that he plans to buy, typically after Christmas during his week off.

Our annual tradition is to gather with Belle and Marty and their sons on Christmas night at our house for dinner. Three years before, during dinner, the discussion turned to the gifts.

"Hey Sam, what did you get this year?" I asked my oldest nephew as I cut into my beef tenderloin.

"Well, from my mom, I got a nice sweater," Sam replied as he chewed his food. "And from Marty I got an envelope. Inside was a four-color picture of a snowboard he plans to buy me."

Katie looked at Sam and then at Marty. "How about you, Belle?" she asked.

"Marty gave me a tracking number," Belle answered, refilling her wine glass.

"A *what*?" asked Katie, in disbelief.

"Hey, hey, kids!" Marty interjected. "Hold on before you pooh-pooh the tracking number. It's actually really cool."

"How so, Marty?" asked Katie.

"Well, for starters, it shows that I actually bought and paid for a present, so it's better than an IOU. Plus, it has the element of anticipation. It's a surprise, and tracking the package is something Belle and I can do together."

Belle rolled her eyes. "Yes. This afternoon, Marty walked me over to the computer, sat me down next to him, placed my hand on the mouse and then put his hand over mine. He insisted that we click on the tracking number together. I don't know what the gift is, but I know it's in Cheyenne, Wyoming right now. It was very romantic."

"See! If you just give a gift, it gets unwrapped and then it's over in like five minutes," Marty reasoned. "This way we get several days of enjoyment out of it."

That Christmas, Sam gave Marty an actual physical gift – a Fitbit wristband. Of course, the Fitbit did not count as a "watch" because it was a health tracking device, despite the fact that it did indeed tell time. In mid-January, after Marty had gotten used to wearing it, we were over at their house for dinner along with one of Katie's brothers, Andy, who is a doctor.

Marty was looking at his Fitbit and showed Andy the app.

"Andy, it says here my resting heart rate is forty-two beats per minute. Could that be right?" asked Marty.

"Well, Marty, you do bike a lot," replied Andy.

"Yeah, but forty-two sounds really low. Is that danger-ous?" asked Marty.

Andy put down his fork and looked at Marty over his glasses. "Marty, you are one of the few people on the planet over fifty years old who doesn't have any stress in their lives whatsoever. There's not a lot of data on people like you. So, yes, it is possible that a fit, stress-free fifty-two year old who has never had a calendar could have a heart rate that low. And no, it is not dangerous."

"Thanks Andy, that's a relief. I think my heart rate jumped to forty-five just thinking about it."

~

Marty is so healthy that he never uses his sick days at school. In over twenty years of teaching, he has used a grand total of four sick days.

One year, Katie and I suggested to Belle and Marty that they join us on a trip to St. John in the U.S. Virgin Islands in April. Belle would be on spring break but Marty would need to take off work.

"Jimbo, the great thing about being a schoolteacher is that you get summers off, and you get a long Christmas break. The bad thing is that you can't really take time off at other times during the year."

"Can you somehow manage three days off in April so we can go to St. John?"

"I'll need to call in sick."

We went ahead and planned the trip. When the day arrived (it was a Saturday), Marty and Belle showed up at the airport and were running late.

"You guys just made it," I commented.

"Yeah, it took us a while to check Belle's bag outside at the curb," said Marty.

"What about your bag?" I asked him.

"This is it." Marty pointed to a small duffel slung over his shoulder, about the size of a gym bag.

"That's it?? What did you pack, Marty?"

We were waiting for our plane to board, so Marty opened up his bag. "Everything I need for five days. Look – a swimsuit, two pairs of shorts, underwear, three T-shirts, toiletries, some food and some sunscreen."

I always knew Marty was a minimalist, but this was extreme. "Lemme see that sunscreen." It looked like it was from the 1950s, but I could find no date on it. "Marty, this has to be expired. How old is this?"

"Jimbo, I'm pretty sure I bought it before they started putting expiration dates on sunscreen. So it's grandfathered in. It will never expire."

Belle and Katie rolled their eyes. "What food do you have?" Katie asked.

Marty rummaged around in his bag and produced something wrapped in plastic about the size of a small football. "A blueberry loaf. It's a good one - from Whole Foods. Want some now?"

"Maybe later. That's it? No more food?" I asked.

"Well, one more thing." Marty dug deep in his bag and brought out a huge plastic bag. "Craisins."

Indeed, it was a 64-ounce Costco-size bag of dried cranberries.

"So Marty, we're headed to an island in the Caribbean, and these are the things you found most necessary to bring along?" Katie asked.

"Well, do you really think we'll be able to find a blueberry loaf or Craisins in St. John?" Marty reasoned.

We flew to St. Thomas and took the ferry over to St. John. We had two great days at the beach, and then got up on Monday morning. Marty had not told anyone he was not going to be in school, so he needed to place the call (I reminded him it was Monday). It was 7:00 a.m.

Marty asked us to be quiet as he dialed the school district number.

"Yes," Marty feigned a cough, gave his name and said. "I...um [cough] need to call in sick today."

The seagulls were squawking in the background. "Yes,

just not feeling well. I [cough] will see how I feel tomorrow. Bye."

Marty hung up the phone, sprung up, clapped his hands, pumped his fists in the air and said, "Okay, kids, let's head to the BEACH!"

29

FALLING WATERS

A bout twenty-five miles into Day 4, we arrived at the small town of Williamsport, Maryland. Here, spanning the entire width of the Potomac, is a dam approximately 700 feet wide and twenty feet high. It was built in 1860 and is used today to generate electricity.

Dam No. 5, Williamsport, MD

A few miles past Williamsport, we started to get hungry.

We remembered the breakfast leftovers Ellen had packed for us, so we pulled our bikes off the trail. A sign caught our eye and we walked across the trail to read it.

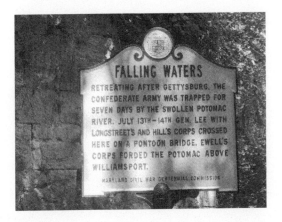

The sign described a significant event that occurred here over 150 years ago.

From July 1–3, 1863, the Confederates under General Robert E. Lee had been defeated at Gettysburg, Pennsylvania by Union Major General George Meade. Lee retreated south – with Meade in pursuit – and arrived at this spot on July 6, hoping to cross over into Virginia. It had been raining heavily, and the water level in the Potomac river was very high. Lee was trapped.

Lincoln wanted Meade to finish Lee off right then and there. But Meade was cautious and waited. Over the next seven days, the river level dropped enough to let the Confederates build a pontoon bridge here, and Lee's army began crossing during the night of July 13th. Meade launched a partial attack the next morning in what became known as the Battle of Falling Waters. But it was too late – Lee had escaped. As a result, the war in Virginia dragged on for nearly two more years.

Later that day, when the news reached Lincoln, he wrote a letter to Meade:

Washington, July 14, 1863

Major General Meade,

... I am very, very grateful to you for the magnificent success you gave the cause of the country at Gettysburg; and I am sorry now to be the author of the slightest pain to you-- But I was in such deep distress myself that I could not restrain some expression of it. I had been oppressed nearly ever since the battles at Gettysburg, by what appeared to be evidences that you... were not seeking a collision with the enemy, but were trying to get him across the river without another battle...

The case, summarily stated is this. You fought and beat the enemy at Gettysburg... He retreated and you did not, as it seemed to me, pressingly pursue him; but a flood in the river detained him... You had at least twenty thousand veteran troops directly with you... and yet you stood and let the flood run down, bridges be built, and the enemy move away at his leisure, without attacking him.

...Again, my dear general, I do not believe you appreciate the magnitude of the misfortune involved in Lee's escape. He was within your easy grasp, and to have closed upon him would, in connection with our other late successes, have ended the war. As it is, the war will be prolonged indefinitely. If you could not safely attack Lee last Monday, how can you possibly do so south of the river? Your golden opportunity is gone, and I am distressed immeasurably because of it.

I beg you will not consider this a prosecution, or persecution of yourself-- As you had learned that I was dissatisfied, I have thought it best to kindly tell you why.

Abraham Lincoln

The letter is viewed as one of the harshest passages Lincoln ever wrote.

However, Meade never actually saw it.

Lincoln never sent the letter, and it was found in the White House after his death.

Lincoln knew that simply venting to Meade would humiliate and de-motivate him at a critical time when he needed Meade the most. Apparently Lincoln did this somewhat frequently as it was his way of coping with frustrating situations.

Marty and I brought out Ellen's leftovers from our bags. We enjoyed her delicious breakfast a second time as we gazed across the Potomac and envisioned Lee's army making their way across, in the middle of the night.

30

ANTIETAM

We mounted our bikes and continued along the path between the canal and the river. Around 1:00 p.m. and fifty-five miles into Day 4, we decided to get off the trail to visit the Antietam Battlefield, site of the bloodiest single-day battle in the Civil War.

Marty and I had been to Antietam about five years earlier. We had spent a week at the Outer Banks with Marty, Belle and their boys, and we were looking for a place to stop to break up the ten-hour drive home. We saw the sign for Antietam and thought it would make for a nice place to take a break while taking in a bit of history.

Our boys were not the least bit interested. In fact, we couldn't even get two of our teenage sons out of the car. After the rest of us toured the battlefield and returned to the parking lot, we asked:

"Boys, why didn't you come and check it out? This place is amazing."

"I hate America," was the sullen response.

This time, Marty and I had a little more time to take in the site at our own pace. We steered our bikes off the C&O

Canal, across Antietam Creek and uphill about two miles to the battlefield. As soon as we emerged from under the tree canopy on the canal, the heat was overwhelming. We parked our bikes and went into the visitor's center, sweaty and covered with mud. The blast of air conditioning immediately gave us relief, and we hit the water fountain. Once inside, we took in a few videos and read some of the literature which told the story of this place.

~

The Battle of Antietam was fought on September 17, 1862, about ten months before Gettysburg and Falling Waters. It occurred approximately eighteen months into the Civil War and resulted in over 22,000 men killed, injured or missing in just twelve hours.

Robert E. Lee crossed the Potomac with his Confederate army on September 10 to begin his invasion of Maryland. They spent a few days encamped outside Frederick, Maryland. After the Confederates left, Union soldiers set up their compound in the same area.

Just before they broke camp, two Union soldiers found a package on the ground containing three cigars. They opened the package only to find the cigars were wrapped in a copy of Lee's orders detailing the Confederate's plan to attack the Union army near Antietam Creek. They quickly passed it up the chain of command and the message was delivered to Union Major General George McClellan, Commander of the Army of the Potomac.

McClellan, mystified by Lee for weeks, now knew his plan. He reportedly gloated: "Here is a paper with which if I cannot whip Bobbie Lee, I will be willing to go home."

However, McClellan was slow to act and missed the

opportunity. He took eighteen hours to set his army in motion. By that point, Lee's intelligence had alerted him to the Union army's moves, and Lee reacted accordingly.

The Cornfield at Antietam

The stage was set just north of Antietam Creek, which Lee crossed the night before the battle and which Marty and I had just crossed on our bikes when leaving the canal trail. The battle started at 5:30 a.m. at Miller's Cornfield, an area about 250 yards deep and 400 yards wide. The field was thick with tall corn stalks and was a perfect hiding place for Confederate soldiers.

As the sun rose, Union Major General Joseph Hooker saw the glint of Confederate bayonets in the Cornfield and ordered his men to enter while his artillery began shelling the field. Men beat each other over the head with rifle butts and stabbed each other with bayonets. With all the shooting, shelling and stabbing, by 9:30 a.m., there were over 13,000 casualties in that small field.

Fighting continued throughout the day, with each side making small gains only to lose ground shortly thereafter.

Although outnumbered two-to-one, Lee had committed all his men, while McClellan sent in about two-thirds of his army, enabling the Confederates to fight the Union to a standstill.

The next day, Lee retreated across the Potomac without resistance from McClellan. This led to Lincoln firing McClellan and replacing him with a series of unsuccessful generals, each of whom lasted just a few months. George Meade, who also fought at Antietam, took over on June 28, 1863, just days before his successful campaign at Gettysburg.

Although tactically inconclusive, the Confederate retreat at Antietam gave Lincoln the confidence to announce his Emancipation Proclamation five days later, which discouraged the British and French governments from pursuing any potential plans to recognize the Confederacy.

~

Marty and I stepped outside back into the heat, fully exposed to the sun. We were at the highest point in the battlefield and could see for miles in every direction. We looked out over the Cornfield – with the stalks nearly as high as they would have been in September – and were amazed that so many men could die so quickly in such a small area. We sensed the gravity of what had happened on these fields over 150 years ago.

We rode our bikes around the entire battlefield. By now it was over ninety degrees and humid. We saw the sites of the other battles, including "Bloody Lane," where 5,500 men perished in the morning in a fierce firefight. We saw many

monuments built as tributes to each of the brigades decimated that day. After about an hour, we were really hot, and
Marty took cover under a tree and sucked on his water bottle.

"We gotta get out of here," he said.

I eased my bike down the hill and joined him under the
tree. "Yeah, it's really hot."

I got out a map and saw what looked to be a shortcut to
getting back to the C&O trail. Marty wanted to simply
retrace our path back to where we originally exited the trail,
but I convinced him to try the shortcut.

We began pedaling out in the heat. What the map did
not show was the changes in elevation on my "shortcut."
The road took us up a huge hill – I made it about halfway up
and then had to walk my bike. During the ascent, the skies
started to darken. Suddenly, a massive thunderstorm
broke out.

We were immediately soaked. Then the lightning
started, and the thunder was deafening. Things went from
uncomfortable to dangerous in less than a minute. After we
crested the top of the hill, we rode our bikes downhill in the
driving rain, looking for cover.

The first building we passed was a dilapidated house
with a covered porch on the front. I had gone on
Appalachian mission trips with my sons for several
summers, and we often worked on houses that looked like
this one. Today, this house would save us.

We decided we needed to get on that porch, no matter
who or what was in the house. Boldly, we carried our bikes
up on the porch and breathed a sigh of relief at being out of
the rain and lightning.

Once we'd caught our breath, we peered in through
the front windows. No sign of life. We knocked on the
door, and a few seconds later, a woman in her fifties came

out, followed by an elderly woman who we quickly determined was her mother. We introduced ourselves and explained our situation. The younger woman, Janet, was extremely gracious and immediately went inside and reappeared with two bottles of ice-cold water – just what we needed!

We told her about our trip. The elderly woman watched us but didn't speak. Janet told us that her mother had dementia. Janet worked at the Maryland state maximum security prison in nearby Hagerstown, Maryland, and began to tell us about some of the prisoners and several harrowing escape attempts. It was a great conversation and a wonderful chance encounter.

As we conversed, the rain eased up and the thunderstorm passed through. We asked Janet about the best way to get back to the C&O Canal trail. She pointed to the route and explained it, which sounded a bit complicated and involved several turns. Marty and I looked at each other and nodded – we were pretty sure we'd got it.

Just before we left, the elderly woman spoke! She said something about the directions to the trail:

"Trail... miss... back up hill... wrong way... long time..."

She was hard to understand, and we tried to make out what she was saying.

"Miss... trail... hill...road... long way back..."

Marty and I could not make sense of her words.

"Hey Mom, these guys need to get on their way," Janet said to her mother dismissively.

We thanked them both, then got on our bikes and headed down the road.

We found the first turn Janet had indicated, and then the second. We headed downhill to what we thought would be the C&O trail. But we saw no sign or indication of the trail.

Then the road started heading uphill, and we followed it for a while – no trail. Marty stopped. I stopped behind him.

"Jimbo, remember what that old lady said?"

"Not really, I couldn't make it out," I replied.

"Something about missing the trail and the road heading back uphill?" said Marty.

"Yeah..."

"I think she was saying that it was easy to miss the trail, and if we missed it, the road would head back uphill and we would end up riding on the road in the wrong direction for a long while," said Marty.

"Yeah, but she didn't know what she was talking about."

"Well, this feels like what she was talking about. Let's head back down."

We aimed our bikes back downhill and, sure enough, we found a small sign marking the trail at the bottom of the hill.

"That old lady was right!" said Marty.

"Probably saved us a bunch of time," I said.

By now, with the Antietam stop, my mis-directions, the rain and the stop on the porch, we were running late. It would be getting dark by the time we'd arrive at our stop for the night. We pedaled hard toward Harpers Ferry.

31

THE BENCH

A s we rode along in the fading sunlight nearing the end of our fourth day, I felt my legs getting tired. I was surprised that it had taken this long for me to feel the effects of what was now a cumulative thirty-five hours on the bike. But I continued to pump my legs. I was glad that Marty had pushed me in training for the ride. I had made a mental note of the total distance I had ridden during our training regimen – it was over 600 miles.

~

One of those training rides had been about a month earlier, in early July. As usual, Marty and I had planned a sixty-mile roundtrip on the Montour Trail. Marty came over to my house in the morning and we headed out. I assumed Marty had already eaten breakfast as I had, and we got on the trail. We banged out the thirty-mile outbound portion in less than three hours.

It was a really hot day. When we started, the temperature was in the high eighties. By 2:00 p.m., on our return trip, it was ninety-five degrees and humid. I noticed Marty slowing down, something I had never seen before. He said he was okay, and so I passed him (a first) and kept going.

After thirty minutes or so, I stopped, got off my bike and waited for him. No Marty. After another ten minutes, I got back on my bike and rode back toward where I had passed him. I saw a biker and asked him if he'd passed a big guy on his bike. He said he had, and told me that the guy was sitting on the side of the trail. I pedaled faster and reached Marty after a couple of miles. He was sitting on a rock on the side of the trail.

"Are you okay?" I asked.

"Yeah, I just didn't eat enough this morning and with this heat, I am going a little slower. I'll be fine."

I didn't have any food to offer him, and he insisted he was okay. We got on our bikes and pedaled slowly. I was actually easing my pace so Marty could keep up with me (another first). After about a mile, Marty got off his bike and sat down on a bench.

"I just need to sit here for a little while," he said.

I was getting worried. "I'm going to get help." I called Katie from my cell phone and told her where we were. We were about five miles from the finish, but about a twenty minute drive from our house. I gave Katie the general location of the bench and told her to bring cold water and some food. At the same time, I got on my bike and pedaled hard for the finish line where I had parked my car. When I got to the end, I jumped in the car and drove back to where I had left Marty. Katie arrived first. When I asked her about it, she described a panicked scene.

"I parked the car where you told me and walked through a couple hundred yards of high grass, eventually getting to the bike trail. I walked along the trail yelling 'Marty! Marty!'

In the distance I spotted the bench with a lifeless figure sprawled out. I ran toward him. He was unconscious!"

The Bench - Montour Trail - Near Mile Marker 25

Marty's recollection is a little different. "I was just taking a nap, and Katie walks up and shakes me and wakes me up."

Katie gave Marty a cold towel for his head and neck, along with two bananas and two cold Perriers (all she could find on short notice). By that time I arrived and Marty was conscious. Katie and I helped get Marty into the car, and he gradually came back to life.

After a few minutes in the car, a thought hit me.

"Marty, did you see what happened there?" I asked.

"What?"

"Marty, you almost died there. Katie came and saved you. She saved your life." I said.

"Yeah, the grim reaper was hovering around that bench," Marty said jokingly.

"Listen to me," I said. "Why do you think Katie would stop what she was doing, grab food and drinks – not to mention cool towels – rush out of our house, speed over here and run down the trail to save you?" I asked.

Marty looked at me quizzically. "Where are you going with this, Jimbo?"

"*Because you are not an asshole!*" I said. "Who goes out of their way to save an asshole's life? If you were an asshole, she would have just rolled her eyes when I called and said something like 'let that asshole die on that bench.' And she would have stayed home, right?"

"You are right!" I could see Marty's energy returning. "Whew - what a relief!"

Marty added: "And you know what else? You kids can rest a little easier because I didn't die. You all get to live another day."

Marty has ridden thousands of miles on his bike, many of them on his own because most people don't have as much free time as he does. I am sure he would have been fine, but I like to think that those Perriers and bananas kept the grim reaper away that day, and kept Belle, Katie and me alive too.

32

A SPECTACULAR CONFLUENCE

J ust before dusk on our fourth day, we arrived at Harpers Ferry, West Virginia. We had completed 274 miles with only sixty-one miles ahead of us.

We had to carry our bikes up a metal staircase in order to reach the bridge which took us into town. This was a daunting task after the long day we'd just had.

Harpers Ferry sits at the confluence of the Potomac and Shenandoah rivers. It is a stunningly beautiful place. The two rivers have carved out huge cliffs over 500 feet high on both sides. Rocks in the rivers create beautiful riffles and the sound of rushing water throughout the town. Here the Shenandoah flows into the Potomac, and the Potomac continues to Washington, DC and eventually to the Chesapeake Bay.

Harpers Ferry is also the place where Virginia, Maryland, and West Virginia converge. You can stand at the tip of Harpers Ferry in West Virginia, while gazing north at Maryland and south at Virginia.

Marty at Harpers Ferry, WV

There is yet another confluence at Harpers Ferry – the C&O Canal trail and the Appalachian Trail intersect here. In fact, the town is near the mid-point of the trail, roughly halfway between Maine and Georgia. The Appalachian Trail typically takes about six months to complete. Hikers often start in the spring at one end and finish in the fall at the other end. In July and August, many of these hikers are halfway through their trek as they pass through Harpers Ferry.

Because of its geographical setting, Harpers Ferry was an important junction point. Beginning in the 1760s, Robert Harper established the first ferry across the Potomac here, and the town became a center of commerce. In 1796, the federal government built the United States Armory and Arsenal at Harpers Ferry, which produced about half of the small arms for the U.S. Army at the time.

Harpers Ferry is best known for John Brown's raid,

during which the first shots of the Civil War were fired. John Brown was an abolitionist who wanted to lead a slave revolt. On October 16, 1859, Brown led a raid on the U.S. arsenal with twenty-one men, five of whom were black. Brown attacked and captured several buildings, hoping to secure the arsenal, arm his men and many other slaves, and start a revolt in Virginia and across the south.

The U.S. sent in a contingent of eighty-six Marines to suppress the raid. Brown was captured, tried for treason and hanged.

Today Harpers Ferry is mostly a tourist town for day-visits from Washington, DC, as well as a spot where hikers and bikers stay. We saw several signs advertising John Brown ghost tours – clearly the locals still profit from that ill-fated raid 150 years ago.

~

When we pulled into Harpers Ferry, the sun was setting. With little daylight left, we quickly made our way uphill to catch a view of the rivers. This took every last bit of energy for me.

At the top of the hill we discovered Jefferson Rock, a large flat piece of shale where Thomas Jefferson stood in October 1783. The view was absolutely stunning.

We could see both the Shenandoah and Potomac rivers and hear the sound of the rippling water below. The majestic, rocky mountains flanked the rivers, and the descending sun created a red glow behind a thin line of clouds just above the top of the cliffs. The air was warm and still humid, and the fireflies were just starting their evening routine, dotting the landscape with brief flashes of light for our viewing pleasure.

View from Jefferson Rock, Harper's Ferry, WV

Thomas Jefferson himself described the view from this spot:

The passage of the Patowmac through the Blue Ridge is perhaps one of the most stupendous scenes in Nature. You stand on a very high point of land. On your right comes up the Shenandoah, having ranged along the foot of the mountain a hundred miles to seek a vent. On your left approaches the Patowmac in quest of a passage also. In the moment of their junction they rush together against the mountain, rend it asunder and pass off to the sea. The first glance of this scene hurries our senses into the opinion that this earth has been created in time, that the mountains were formed first, that the rivers began to flow afterwards, that in this place particularly they have been so dammed up by the Blue Ridge of mountains as to have formed an ocean which filled the whole valley... The piles of rock on each hand, but particularly on the Shenandoah, the marks of their disruptions and avulsions from their beds by the most powerful agents in nature, corroborate the impression.

Thomas Jefferson, Notes on the State of Virginia, 1785

I couldn't have said it better myself.

We pulled ourselves away from the view, eased our bikes downhill back into town and parked them in front of the Harper Hotel, our home for the last night of our trip.

At the hotel, we checked in with Wanda, who was in her sixties with long gray hair and wore a long black gown. She showed us to our room upstairs – two large beds and a shared bath down the hall. She told us that there was a canteen with snacks and drinks in her office, and we could help ourselves and leave money to pay for whatever we took.

We showered and then headed out to get something to eat. It had been a long day on the trail and we were hungry. Central Harpers Ferry is very small and there are just a few restaurants. We found one that looked good – I opted for seafood pasta and Marty had a burger. We left satisfied and headed back to the hotel.

As we returned to the hotel, a small group of people were sitting in the dark just below the entrance. Holding court in front of this group was a man dressed as John Brown, complete with Civil War-era clothing and a wig. He was telling his story of that October day in 1859 when he led the raid on the arsenal, captivating his audience of five people. It was funny, odd and creepy at the same time. We headed up to our room.

Before we settled into our beds, I realized I wanted a bottle of water. I remembered the canteen Wanda had told us about in her office, and I headed downstairs. It was late and everything was pitch dark. I let my eyes adjust and was able to make out the outline of the office, which now had a heavy curtain pulled across the entrance. I pulled back the curtain and started to walk in when I saw a figure lying on the bench inside the office. As I got closer, I realized it was

Wanda! She rolled over and squinted at me. I panicked and ran out of the office, back up the steps and arrived into our room out of breath.

"Jimbo, did you get your water?"

"Uh... no."

"Why not?"

"Well, that lady... Wanda... *she sleeps in the office!*"

"What?"

"Yeah, I saw her. It was dark and she was sleeping in there. It was really creepy so I left. I don't need the water."

"That's weird."

"Yeah, let's get some sleep and get outta here tomorrow."

We slept well. The next morning, it was pouring rain. The Harper Hotel was serving breakfast on a covered deck, and a number of Appalachian Trail hikers were there. They had come to get a night or two off the trail and stay with a roof over their heads and dry out.

Each one of them had an interesting story. Since it takes half a year to hike the trail, a common thread was that they all had the time to devote to this adventure. One woman, Jessica, was a lawyer from Los Angeles who had been let go from her job. She had always wanted to do the hike but had never really hiked or camped before. So she bought the gear and flew to Maine and got started.

Jessica said that after several weeks, trail hikers realize that every extra pound on their backs makes a difference. She started getting rid of things she didn't need, and three months into the hike she was down to the bare essentials.

Jessica told us of encounters she'd had with bears, rattlesnakes and other wildlife - all by herself. But she said that she'd been disappointed with many of the people she met on the trail. She said many were anarchists who would carve swastikas on trees! She said the conversation we had with her was one of the most "normal" conversations she had had in three months.

The rain had stopped and the sun was coming out. We packed up, got on our bikes, and headed back to the C&O trail.

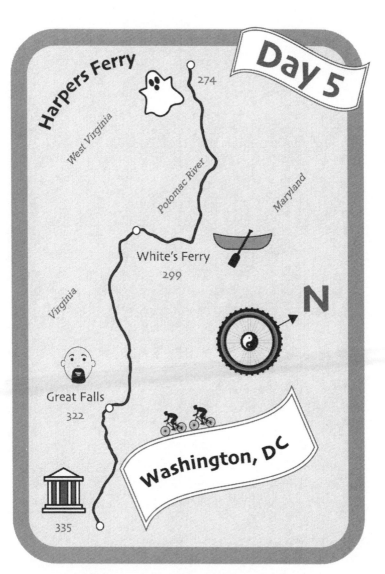

Harpers Ferry, WVa to Washington, DC

33

THE CHAIRS

As we began the last day of our trip, I was feeling tired. Without any recovery time in between long rides each day, my legs and butt were sore. I continued to be amazed at how easy this seemed for Marty.

Actually, for Marty, this type of trail riding is significantly less strenuous than mountain biking. He has several friends with whom he rides in the hills around Pittsburgh every Sunday – Chris (who was injured in Frick Park), Jamey and Jack. I have joined them a few times but have a hard time keeping up.

After they finish their ride – typically by around noon – Marty breaks out a cooler of beer and folding chairs from his car and they sit around and drink beer for two or three hours before heading back home. This essentially consumes the rest of the day.

Marty's friend Jack has three young daughters. Jack's girls are involved in sports and lots of other activities, so he is a busy dad on the weekends. For Jack, spending an entire Sunday afternoon sitting in a parking lot in the woods drinking beer is hard to justify to his wife.

As Marty and I rode along the canal together, Marty was riding fast and I was working hard trying to keep his pace.

"Jimbo, you should come out mountain biking with us again sometime," Marty said.

"I can't keep up with you guys."

"Did I tell you about what happened last weekend with Jack?" Marty asked.

"I don't think so." I was panting while Marty was barely exerting any energy.

"So last Sunday, Jack came over to my house to meet up for a ride. I made cappuccinos and we were loading up my car to drive out to the mountains," Marty said.

"Nice."

Marty continued: "So get this. I needed to go back into my house to get my air pump, and Jack stayed at the car. I came back out to the car, opened the lift gate to put the pump in, and the first thing I notice is that my chairs are gone."

"Okay..."

"Yeah," Marty chuckled. "I knew those chairs were in there. So I walked back to the garage and, sure enough, I found them leaning up against the wall. Can you believe Jack took them out and thought I wouldn't notice?"

Marty was now howling laughing as he continued the story, gesturing with both hands as he lifted them off the handlebars.

"So I picked up the chairs and walked back to the car and held them up to Jack. You should have seen the look on his face. He said something like 'Oh... Marty... we almost forgot them!' He was so busted," Marty said mockingly.

Jack knows Marty as well as I do. He knows that Marty requires a sitting position to drink beer for long periods of time. Jack had reasoned that without the chairs, Marty would not want to stay very long. And if the chairs weren't there, Marty would simply think he forgot to pack them in the car.

What Jack didn't know was that Marty always keeps those chairs in his car, because at any given moment the opportunity to sit and drink beer may present itself.

34

FAT OR BALD?

From Harpers Ferry it is exactly sixty-one miles to DC. We pedaled along, and I was looking forward to ending the day on the Mall and seeing my parents.

The bike trail was set between the C&O Canal and the Potomac River - to our left was the canal, and to the right was the river. As we continued downstream, the Potomac got wider, and the canal was also wide and beautiful. We frequently saw turtles and Great Blue Herons in the canal.

About twenty-five miles past Harpers Ferry, we arrived at White's Ferry, the last of the nearly one hundred ferries that once operated on the Potomac River. Positioned at a calm stretch in the river, this ferry shuttles up to twenty cars and their passengers back and forth on a flat, open boat running along a wire cable. We had taken this ferry several times on New Year's Eve when we lived in Maryland and celebrated the holiday with Katie's brother in Leesburg, Virginia. It was always eerie coming back across the river in the pitch dark, and we had to monitor the weather because when there is ice in the river, the ferry does not operate.

From the late 1800s, the ferry boat bore the name Jubal A. Early, named after a prominent Confederate General during the Civil War who led troops in a number of key battles in the Eastern Theater. After the war, Early fled to Mexico, then Cuba and finally Canada. When he eventually returned to the United States in 1870, he was a leader in the Lost Cause movement, an ideology which held that the Confederates' cause was noble and just, and that slavery in fact was also justified because it brought economic prosperity. His name was removed from the ferry in the summer of 2020.

I had never been to White's Ferry in the summertime, and we found it to be a beautiful spot. Marty and I grabbed a couple of Diet Cokes and Snicker's bars in the snack shop, parked our bikes under a tree and watched the ferry load up and make its slow trip across the river to Virginia.

To our left, just downstream, a large, flat island sits in the middle of the Potomac. The river divides into two parts as it skirts around the atoll – known as Harrison Island – and then rejoins in full strength as it makes its way toward Great Falls. On the Virginia side, Ball's Bluff rises above the river, covered with trees all the way up the embankment.

Katie's brother lives just beyond the bluff, and on one visit we hiked out to the top of this cliff from his house. The combination of the island and the bluff makes for a serene and lovely scene, but on October 21, 1861, it is safe to say that no one was paying much attention to this view.

≈

Three months after the start of the Civil War, the Union had determined it was important to gain control of Leesburg. Harrison Island looked to be a good place to cross the Potomac, since it meant fording two smaller forks rather than taking on the entire expanse of the river. During the night of October 20, 1861, the Union army crossed the first segment, scrambled over Harrison Island, then crossed the second segment and worked their way up to the top of Ball's Bluff. They were surprised by the Confederates the next morning as they counter-attacked, driving the Union troops back over the bluff and into the Potomac, firing into the backs of the soldiers attempting to swim away.

≈

Fortunately, the only adversaries Marty and I faced today were hunger, heat and humidity. Energized from our snacks, we mounted our bikes and got back on the C&O towpath. After White's Ferry, the trail was straight and flat, and Marty wanted to do some fast riding. I told him to go ahead and I would catch up with him at Great Falls. I rode by myself for about two hours, taking in the spectacular views of the Potomac.

Jim riding the C&O Canal trail at White's Ferry

Twenty miles later I arrived at Great Falls. Here the Potomac narrows and there are massive boulders in the river, creating thundering rapids. Huge rock walls on the Virginia side attract climbers and rapellers. In fact, I had rappelled there with my son's cub scout troop ten years before.

The Potomac River at Great Falls

Great Falls contains a few structures, including a tavern from the 1800s, now converted to a gift shop. Great Falls also is the site of a still-functioning lock, and here lock workers in period costumes present a re-enactment whereby they open and close the lock and lower a boat.

I found a soda machine and bought a bottle of water, then proceeded to look around for Marty. I found him sitting on a bench in the shade. I pedaled over and planted myself next to him. It was nearly ninety degrees and getting progressively more humid as we got closer to DC. It felt good to get out of the sun.

We sat and watched the actors work the lock, which was a very intricate and time-consuming operation. As we watched, our minds wandered.

"Jimbo, have you noticed we haven't seen a lot of fat or bald people riding on the trail?" Marty posed an interesting question I had not considered until now.

"Yeah, you're right. Well, it takes a lot of training to pull off what we're doing. Fat people probably just can't do it," I responded. The actors gently pulled the boat into the top of the lock using ropes and closed the gate behind it.

"Yes, but you don't see a lot of bald people either," said Marty, sipping on his drink.

"True," I played along. "I don't know why that would be."

"Fatness and baldness tend to go together, don't you think?" Marty was on to something.

"Yes, come to think of it – Don Rickles, Winston Churchill, George Costanza..."

"Buddha..." Marty chimed in.

"Wimpie..." I added.

The actors opened the baffles on the bottom of the lock. Water began rushing from the top to the bottom and the boat lowered along with the water level.

"I wonder what comes first... are you fat first, and then lose your hair? Or bald first and then you get fat?" Marty asked.

"Well, my guess is that if you're bald, you tend to let yourself go, and you kind of give up. And then you end up fat." I was giving this some serious thought.

"Maybe." Marty was considering the alternative. "But

maybe you are fat first, and then somehow being overweight causes you to lose your hair. And then you end up bald."

"Good point," I concurred. "Well, either way, you don't see many of them out here."

Once the water level had equalized on the bottom of the lock, the actors pulled open the gate and used the ropes to pull the boat out of the lock and down the canal. Mission accomplished.

35

FINISH LINE

few miles past Great Falls, we hit a paved section – the Capital Crescent trail – which took us all the way to Georgetown. After pedaling for five days, I was home.

We passed many familiar places which brought back great memories of growing up here. Just past Chain Bridge, I spotted the stretch of the canal where my dad had taken us ice skating when it froze over in the early 1970s. Next we passed Fletcher's Boat House, where I drank beers with my friends in high school.

Looking to my right, I saw the Three Sisters Islands in the Potomac. We then went under the Key Bridge, a concrete arch bridge over which I'd driven hundreds of times going from my home in Arlington to Georgetown. We skirted around Washington Harbour, passing the familiar scene of people dining outside at Tony & Joe's.

The trail led us between the river and the Kennedy Center, where Katie's sister Tish held her wedding reception. We followed it all the way to West Potomac Park, where I had practiced with my Gonzaga High School soccer team nearly every weekday in the fall.

Next we arrived on the Mall in DC. The Washington Monument, the Lincoln Memorial, Jefferson Memorial, all packed with tourists from around the world on this hot, humid August day. Our shirts were covered in mud from the trail. We got off our bikes in front of the Lincoln Memorial and asked someone to take a picture of us.

The Finish Line – Lincoln Memorial, Washington, DC

We walked up the steps and into the memorial. Inside is a seated Lincoln, looking out over the reflecting pool and toward the Washington Monument. To his right, the Gettysburg Address is etched into the marble.

Lincoln delivered this famous speech on November 19, 1863 at the commemoration of the cemetery at the Gettysburg battlefield, fourteen months after the Battle of Antietam. While Antietam was the single bloodiest day of the Civil War, Gettysburg was a three-day battle that cost the most lives of all Civil War battles – 58,000 men. Lincoln delivered the address with a goal of ending the war.

"Fourscore and seven years ago our fathers brought forth, on this continent, a new nation, conceived in liberty, and dedicated to the proposition that all men are created equal.

Now we are engaged in a great civil war, testing whether that nation, or any nation so conceived, and so dedicated, can long endure. We are met on a great battle-field of that war. We have come to dedicate a portion of that field, as a final resting-place for those who here gave their lives, that that nation might live.

It is altogether fitting and proper that we should do this. But, in a larger sense, we cannot dedicate, we cannot consecrate—we cannot hallow—this ground. The brave men, living and dead, who struggled here, have consecrated it far above our poor power to add or detract.

The world will little note, nor long remember what we say here, but it can never forget what they did here. It is for us the living, rather, to be dedicated here to the unfinished work which they who fought here have thus far so nobly advanced. It is rather for us to be here dedicated to the great task remaining before us—that from these honored dead we take increased devotion to that cause for which they here gave the last full measure of devotion—that we here highly resolve that these dead shall not have died in vain—that this nation, under God, shall have a new birth of freedom, and that government of the people, by the people, for the people, shall not perish from the earth."

Abraham Lincoln's Gettysburg Address
November 19, 1863

Marty and I absorbed the significance of this piece of

history. It seemed to us ironic and sad that not much has changed in 150 years. In the 1860s we were a nation divided – black vs white, slave vs free, north vs south. Today, after the Civil War, two world wars, thirty additional presidents and the building of hundreds of monuments, we are still a nation divided. We had just ridden our bikes through over 300 miles of relatively poor Appalachian communities, all working hard and paying taxes, only to arrive at the gleaming capitol of our nation, everything pristinely clean and white. Having grown up in Washington, my father a career Federal civil servant, I had never really appreciated this disconnect until now.

Well, enough of the heavy stuff – we were ready for a beer! We got back on our bikes and headed over the Memorial Bridge into Virginia, with Arlington Cemetery in front of us. We entered the Fort Myer Army base, where our family would watch the fireworks on the Fourth of July and dine in the Officer's Club on Sundays for brunch. The sergeant let us in through the gate and we wound our way through the base, past the Officer's Club and other familiar sites. We exited the base on the other side and passed the recreation center where I played basketball with my brothers when we were kids.

We crossed Arlington Boulevard and headed into the neighborhood where I grew up and where my parents still lived. Everything felt familiar and, riding my bike, it felt like old times. It had just taken me five days to get here and I was exhausted!

We headed up the driveway and parked our bikes. Then we walked up the stairs and knocked on the door. My Mom came to the door and greeted us.

"Well look at you guys!" We were filthy, hot and thirsty. Mom immediately produced some cold beers.

Jim and Mom at her house in Arlington, VA

Just then, Belle arrived in her van. Mom made us all a wonderful pasta dinner.

We told them about the trip, from the lady with foreign accent syndrome in Connellsville to the amazing milkshakes in Meyersdale to Bill's Place in Little Orleans. We laughed and had a great time.

Marty and I slept well that night. The next morning, Belle drove us back to Pittsburgh. Watching the landscape go by at 65 mph was quite different than at 12 mph. We were home in four hours.

36

REAL LIFE

L ife got back to normal fairly quickly. Marty went back to teaching school at the end of August, and I started a new job in September. My calendar filled back up with appointments and business trips. But I retained one thing from my time off with Marty – I left the watch in my dresser drawer. I had gotten used to life without it and kind of liked it.

I didn't ride the bike much after that. The trip had worn me out, and while I loved it, I was ready for a break. I would look at the bike in my garage every now and then and it would remind me of those days on the trail.

Marty, however, continued to ride his bike nearly every day. One day that fall we were over at Belle and Marty's house for dinner. Marty and I walked through his garage where he keeps his bikes – about seven or eight of them in a row, hung from the ceiling on hooks – mountain bikes, road bikes and trail bikes. I was inspecting the array of cycles and spotted one I had not seen before.

"Marty, what is this one?" I asked.

"That's a full-suspension mountain bike. It has shock absorbers in the front and rear – it's for really rough trails."

"I haven't seen it before. Is it new?" It was an impressive, high end piece of equipment.

"Yeah, I just got it. A friend of mine gave it to me," Marty said.

I thought about this for a moment. "Your friend just *gave* it to you?" I asked. "For no particular reason?"

"Yeah. Pretty nice, huh?"

"You know, Marty," I said. "You know what this means, right?"

"What, Jimbo?" asked Marty, looking up at the bike.

"Think about it..."

Marty thought, then winked, nodded and started laughing. "That's good stuff, Jimbo."

When we'd get together that fall and during the winter, we would reminisce about the bike trip and re-tell the stories. Katie and Belle got tired of hearing them. As spring-time came and the weather started warming up, Marty talked about doing it again. I told him that due to my job, I probably couldn't pull off both a beach trip and a bike trip in the same summer. Marty was bummed.

"Jimbo, that job of yours is really getting in the way."

School ended in mid-June, and Marty once again began his annual three-month vacation. Belle and Marty came over one Saturday for dinner in late June. As Marty walked in, I asked him:

"Marty, have you lost track of days yet? Do you know what day it is?"

"Well, I have a pretty good idea. It's either Saturday or Sunday," Marty replied.

"How do you know?" asked Katie.

"'Cause Jimbo's home. Jimbo's home on Saturdays and Sundays." We had a good laugh.

That night the four of us played cards. I sat across the table from Marty and something on his arm caught my attention. There, on his wrist, was something I had never seen before on Marty – a *watch*.

"Marty – what's that on your wrist??"

Marty looked down and was slightly embarrassed. "Yeah, I know."

"*Why are you wearing a watch?*" I was perplexed. "Last summer you educated me on the benefits of not wearing a watch, and look, I'm still not wearing one."

Marty tried to explain: "Well, in the classroom, the kids are always asking me what time it is. Since there isn't a clock in the room, I broke down and got a watch. It's not for me, it's for them."

"I don't know what to say," I said. "Things have really changed. It's like a paradigm shift."

Marty got a little agitated and dropped his cards on the table. He raised his voice a bit. "Well, Jimbo, I may have a watch, but you have a *job*. And that job is keeping you from biking."

Marty continued: "Look, I can take this watch off any time I want." He removed his watch with an exaggerated gesture and set it down on the table. "Look, no more watch." Then he pointed his finger at me. "*But you still have that job!*"

I felt a little dejected. He was right. But I realized in that moment that even though I had a job, I could still fit in a bike trip. Without even asking me to "see what I could do," Marty had convinced me to do it again.

I went down into the garage the next day and got the bike out. And two months later we were on the trail to DC again!

AFTERWORD

by Marty

(I saw what I could do!)

I hope you have enjoyed this little book of stories shared between friends traveling through life together. From my perspective, this book is about two things – first, the sheer joy of riding a bicycle and second, how special it is to have a true, genuine friendship with someone. Jim and I have combined these, and our shared experiences have resulted in a lifetime of memories which we now share with you.

To the first point: The sheer joy of riding a bicycle. The adventures described herein were made possible by hopping on a bicycle and being open to the encounters that occur organically while on the road. Riding the Great Allegheny Passage (GAP) is a pleasure beyond measure. The greenery, the fresh and scented air, the many rippling rivers, the rhythmic sound of bike tires on the crushed limestone surface, and the exhilaration that comes from physical fitness combine to elevate mind, body, and soul. These simple pleasures are made possible to anyone, regardless of ability, to experience by simply riding a bicycle.

To the second point: True friendship. It is in this heightened state that Jim and I pedaled along on our ride to Washington, DC, meeting people, telling stories, revisiting old memories while making new ones, laughing, enjoying life, being open to the moment, and being together. While Jim has emphasized some of my character traits including observation, it should be clear that he too is a keen observer of all that life presents to him. Jim's passion for life is easily recognized in the telling of the stories you have just read. This is what I most admire about him. I always am made to feel a better person when I am with him. I am honored and blessed to call him my friend.

I encourage you to join a friend and take on a similar cycling adventure for yourself and create lifelong memories of your own. The Great Allegheny Passage is waiting for you!

ACKNOWLEDGMENTS

My mom told me that books typically contain a section at the end where the author thanks the people who helped him or her out. So here goes.

Although my name is on the cover, this book was a total family project and a labor of love which we have thoroughly enjoyed over the last couple of years. While publishing it is rewarding, the real reward has been all the laughs and fun we've had while creating it.

First, I would like to thank Belle for being excited about the book from the beginning, for spending countless hours on all the artwork and layout, for her feedback and editing, and for reading the book aloud to Marty. Otherwise, he would probably still not know the contents of the book.

I would like to thank my mom for her encouragement, for tons of feedback and editing, and for being patient in raising a non-reading son. Mom has known Marty as long as I have. She once said: "I absolutely love Marty. He is hilarious and is one of my favorite people. But I could never be married to him." (Belle - thanks for doing that, too).

I would like to thank Katie for her constant love and

support, for putting up with me working on this book, for her editing, and for being willing to let me spend one of my two weeks of annual vacation on a bike trip with Marty.

Finally, I would like to thank Marty for being a great friend (after all, who would write an entire book about another person if that person is an...?). Marty has helped me learn how to slow down, live in the moment and appreciate the little things. He has shown me that life is about the journey and not the destination. And if you open yourself up to new experiences and meeting new people, you never know what might be around the next bend.

INDEX OF GAP/C&O TOWNS VISITED

RESOURCES

Please review the book on Goodreads or Amazon - thanks!

Continue the discussion! More Jim & Marty stories and videos are on Facebook at
Facebook.com/GetUpAndRideBook

Visit our website and sign up for our **monthly newsletter** for videos, stories, events and book club information:
www.GetUpRide.com

A portion of the book proceeds are donated to support the Great Allegheny Passage and Montour Trail. For information visit **gaptrail.org** and **montourtrail.org**

We want to hear from you!
To contact the author, or to party with Marty,
email **GetUpRide@gmail.com**

ABOUT THE AUTHOR

Jim Shea is a tech sales & marketing executive and sporadic cyclist. This is Jim's first book. Jim's career has taken him from the Washington DC area to Silicon Valley to his current home in Pittsburgh, PA. He enjoys spending time with his wife, Katie, their three adult sons, and extended family and friends.

Jim also plays acoustic guitar and sings folk, classic rock and contemporary Christian music. He attended the University of Notre Dame (GO IRISH!) and Stanford Business School.

Jim and Marty have cycled the Great Allegheny Passage and C&O Canal three times and are currently contemplating their next adventure.

EARLY PRAISE FOR "GET UP AND RIDE"

"It's great Jimmy. Since you don't read books, you haven't been influenced by great authors such as Steinbeck or Hemingway. It reads just like you talk – it's your *own style.*"
– Mom

"Nice work Jimbo. If you publish it, I'll buy a copy!"
– Marty

"It's actually pretty good."
– Katie (wife)

"Jimmy, the other good thing about it is that it is short. People like books that don't take too long to read."
– Mom

"I wet my pants."
– Mary (sister-in-law)

"It's easy. You don't have to think too hard when you read it."
– Ellie (niece)

"You *wrote* a book? Since when did you start reading books? I don't know who you are anymore."
– John (brother)

"Wow, you really spent over 100 hours working on that, Dad?"
– Thomas (son)

Made in the USA
Columbia, SC
10 January 2023

75812769R00121